# Psycho Too

# Psycho Too

Words by Will Self

Pictures by Ralph Steadman

BLOOMSBURY

LONDON · BERLIN · NEW YORK

First published in Great Britain 2009

Text copyright © by Will Self 2003, 2004, 2005, 2006, 2007, 2008, 2009
Illustrations copyright © Ralph Steadman 2003, 2004, 2005, 2006, 2007, 2008, 2009

Author, artist and publisher gratefully acknowledge that with the exception of the introduction and its images, all the other words and pictures in this book were first published in the *Independent* newspaper in their 'Psychogeography' column between 2003 and 2008

Bloomsbury Publishing Plc
36 Soho Square, London WID 3QY

www.bloomsbury.com

Bloomsbury Publishing, London, New York and Berlin

A CIP catalogue record for this book is available from the British Library

ISBN 978 1 4088 0228 1
10 9 8 7 6 5 4 3 2 1

Printed in Singapore by Tien Wah Press
Text design and typesetting by Polly Napper

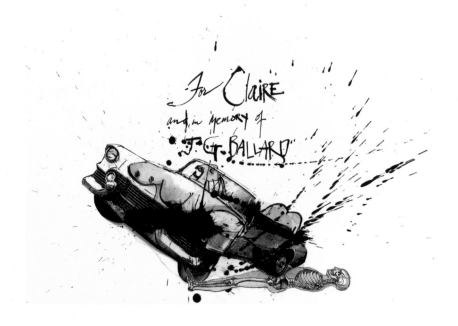

For Claire
and in memory of
"J. G. BALLARD"

# Contents

# Walking to The World

I decided to walk to The World from J. G. Ballard's house in Shepperton. Jim had been in hospital over Christmas – the chemical refinery of the Hammersmith, which faces out over the veldt-in-*urb* of Wormwood Scrubs – and the experience had nearly done for him. 'They were suggesting he move to a single room at the end of the ward,' said Claire, his girlfriend, 'and you *know* what that means.' Of course I did: 90 per cent of the spending on healthcare in any given English individual's life takes place in the last six weeks of life, up until then welfare provision may have been patchy, but a citizen's final demise is invariably on full-board and en suite – assuming, that is, express checkout.

Claire extracted Jim from the hospital and took him back to her flat in Shepherd's Bush. I could picture the rhythms of this phase of their lives together, the coming and going of the district nurse, the pitter-patter of tiny pills. When I spoke to Claire on the phone she remained simply delighted to have wrested him from the clutches of hospital medicine – with its all too often pointless heroism – and to have restored him to a domestic context. Ballard, the most outlandish of fictional imaginers, had always dug out his wellspring by the hearth, and remained the perfect exemplar of Flaubert's dictum: a bourgeois in his life, a revolutionary in his dreams.

Claire worked at her computer during the days, a baby alarm next to her mouse mat so she could hear if he needed anything, then, when it was time to go to bed she took it with her. 'When I take it upstairs,' she wrote to me, 'it's as if I'm carrying his breathing self in the little plastic machine. I hold it very carefully in my hand, like a precious living thing . . . (I haven't told him).' I found this quite unbearably affecting; indeed, I had become involved in all of this in a way I found both difficult to understand – and painfully obvious.

I had propped up a copy of Jim's memoir *Miracles of Life* on the bookcase in the kitchen, so that each morning, on coming downstairs, I was met by the image of the child Ballard, riding his tricycle in Shanghai. I felt myself opening out to the numinous in my communion with the dying writer, an intimation of alternate realities, including, perhaps, some in which we had been as close emotionally – and physically – as we had been imaginatively; for, to pretend to an intimate relationship with Jim would've been presumptuous – we had met at most five or six times.

The first had been in 1994, when Ballard was publishing *Rushing to Paradise*, his warped eco-parable version of *The Tempest*, wherein Greenpeace activists and South Seas sybarites run amok on an atoll used for nuclear weapons testing. Like so many before me, I had made the pilgrimage to the Surrey dormitory town of Shepperton to interview its sage for a newspaper. All was as has been described in scores of articles: the neat little semi along the somnolent suburban street, the mutant yucca straining against the curved mullions of the front window, the Ford Granada humped in the driveway. Inside, the small rooms were dominated by the reproductions of lost Paul Delvaux nudes that Jim had commissioned himself; other than this oddity the decor was an exercise in unconcern – and not a studied one.

'Would you like a drink?' he asked, vigorous in an open-necked white shirt. 'I've got *everything*.'

I had had, of course, a fantasy of quaffing Scotch with Ballard – I knew of his legendary and unashamed consumption: the first tumbler poured in the morning when he returned from the school run, the leisurely topping-up throughout the writing day, two-fingers-per-hour, clackety-clack, as his fingers gouged their way into inner space. However, like a lot of alcoholics I couldn't risk taking a drink in the afternoon – especially if I was working – the comedown was instant, I would have to have more – and more; no leisurely sousing but a sudden spirituous down-pour, so I asked, 'Can I have a cup of tea?'

Jim grimaced: 'Too much trouble, boiling water and things . . .' he gestured vaguely.

I settled for water. We sat down in the back sitting room, looking out through French windows to a sunlit garden. Jim chortled, 'So, you've managed to extricate yourself from that cocaine-smuggling business have you?'

He was referring to a recent bust I'd had for possessing hashish in the Orkney Islands, where I'd been living up until a couple of months previously – the case had recently been heard at the Sheriff Court in Kirkwall, and made a few column inches down south. I explained the situation – but he seemed utterly uninterested in the detail: possession/supply, hash/coke – it was, his manner suggested, all one to him. I found myself strangely bothered by how *dégagé* Ballard was, as if it was his responsibility to either condemn or condone my actions. It was absurd; true, he was thirty-one years my senior – but I was a grown man, besides, he wasn't my father; or, at least, not biologically.

For that was the problem, as well as the abiding infantilism of my own malaise – the need to blame everyone else for my own derelictions, my ethical pratfalls and emotional incontinence – I also believed I was Ballard's mind-child, that my hypertrophied creative impulse had burst from his domed forehead, slathering his remaining greyish hair with amniotic fluid. It's a sensitive business, this one of literary patrimony – although I'd never had any anxiety about my influences. There were those writers whose work spoke to me, those whose mannerisms, tropes, accidents of style were – in Auden's memorable acronym – GETS, 'Good Enough to Steal' – and then there were a very select few who had carved out the conceptual space within which I sought to stake my own claim. Of these, Ballard was the pre-eminent.[*]

The great wind from nowhere of October 1987: I awoke in a sepia dawn to a cacophony of tortured metal; through the Venetian blind slats I could see that six by three-foot panels of corrugated iron were being torn from the scaffolding on the old LCC block opposite. The zephyr was strong enough to be holding some upright and push them along the road surface, striking sparks. Nature, kept away from the city by its mighty radiation – repelled by roofs, walls and fences – had broken through. Except that in this mundane urban context the wind – no matter how strong – could not possibly be from nowhere, only a little further north, say Camden Town.

I associate my Ballardian apprenticeship with this period, in my middle twenties, when, recently sprung from four months in rehab, I shared a flat on the Barnsbury Road in Islington with an elfin would-be mime artist. We painted the floors red and listened to southern soul on an antiquated valve record player;

---

* 'I christened the new terrain I wished to explore "inner space", that psychological realm (manifest, for example, in surrealist painting) where the inner world of the mind and the outer world of reality meet and fuse.' J. G. Ballard, *Crash* (1974), Introduction to the French edition.

occasionally my flatmate did a handspring – a manoeuvre he had used to evade the bulls in Pamplona.

I was nervy and racked by caffeine and nicotine – one morning I even *overdosed* on coffee, no mean achievement. I had a writerly girlfriend who was more advanced than me – she'd actually completed a novel, and in due course it was published. I found it difficult to get *at* her: after sweaty midnights, then throughout those cold dawns I struggled to prise apart her thin and resistant white limbs. I recall the feel of hand-me-down parental linen – and sinking into the trough of a broken-backed bed dragged back from the furniture warehouse on the Liverpool Road. She turned away from my carefully crafted caresses and I saw peculiar spiral markings on her bare back and stubby neck. Ring worm. We both had it – the vermiculation of our short-let accommodation had bored through the plaster and into our flesh.

For a vermifuge we read *Crash*, and savoured its opening lines: 'Vaughan died yesterday in his last car-crash. During our friendship he had rehearsed his death in many crashes, but this was his only true accident.' This said it all; the intersection between the performative and the desperate – the gargantuan alienation of the modern machine/man matrix trumped by a studied act of self-violence. When we were out, driving in her Renault 5 van, she would grab hold of my arm, yanking the steering wheel. 'Crash!' she'd exhale in my ear. 'Crash!' I'd breathe back – and this was the best consummation we ever managed, except for one cold afternoon coupling in the back of the van.

We had driven out from London to the Isle of Grain in the Thames estuary. Since an epiphany experienced the previous summer on a sunlit street in Mayfair I had spent more and more time cruising the periphery of London: how was it that I had never visited – nor even envisaged – the mouth of the river that ran through my natal city? And so I was drawn to those desolate places where redundant heavy industry was sinking into the mire between retail barns and business parks: Erith Marsh, Thamesmead, Tilbury – and eventually the Ultima Thule of Grain itself, where the cracked pavements were sutured with weeds and the rust-streaked pipe-lines of the oil refinery snaked through the marsh grasses. The necrotic flesh of plastic bags flapped on barbed-wire fences, crows descended on the corpse of a muddy field, seagulls followed the plough, pylons engaged in a tug of war with high-tension cables, and the cloud piled up over Sheppey, black upon grey. In the dully humbling cul-de-sacs of the last council estate in southern England a child's bicycle lay unclaimed on an un-mown verge; beyond the concrete baffler of the seawall the Maunsell Towers strode towards the horizon, like Wells's Martian tripods.

On these forays into the interzones I took photographs, and made cryptic notes that no one – not even me – would ever read again. I felt myself to be engaged in some crucial project: the discovery of an essential reality that remained inviolate, incapable of being assimilated to the marketable portions of locale and territory into which the land was being subdivided. This was no village England, or rural idyll, nor could it be incorporated into the smoothly-functioning machinery of the conurbation, where built environment, transportation and humanity all played their part in the Taylorisation of space.

On the muddy foreshore below the village of Grain there were cracked dragon's teeth, and an old stone causeway, greasy-green with seaweed, that led out to Grain Tower, a Second World War gun emplacement. I piloted the Renault along the rough track beneath an embankment protecting the power station from the Medway. Freighters came drifting in on the tide, their superstructures as high and white and rectangular as blocks of flats. I stopped the car and – terribly aroused – made my slinky moves.

That brisk March day the sex was probably no great shakes – only the usual soft rasp and toothy snag; but the ridged metal of the van's floor, the awkward positions we had to assume in order to fit – one into the other, both into the abbreviated compartment – these were thrillingly hard correlates of the interzone that lay beyond the Renault's double doors: we were fucking the furnaces and cooling towers, the generators and coal hoppers. Our breathy spasms and cramped ejaculations reverberated against the chilled earth and the aching sky. On the way back to London we bought a cheese and pickle sandwich at a petrol station and as we shared it the yellow-white gratings dropped into our laps like the shredded skin of H-bomb victims. I had her stained underwear stuffed in the pocket of my jacket.

The relationship staggered on for another nine months; then, at the beginning of 1988, my mother arrived punctually at the terminal stages of cancer. Each day I went to her flat in Kentish Town to give her sublingual morphine sulphate and other, more cack-handed ministration. Perhaps, facing this enormity, I was too needy – or maybe my girlfriend's neediness was now insupportable; one or the other, it was no longer enough for her to yank my arm and implore me to 'Crash!' I *was* crashing. We had read Ballard together, there had been the sex on the Isle of Grain – and that was enough: *The Atrocity Exhibition*, *Vermillion Sands*, *Hello America* – books I had initially consumed in my early teens, when I used to guzzle up the quintuple-decker sandwiches of science fiction I carried back from East Finchley library (rubber-soled sneakers squeaking on the polished floors, the deferential hush now long since sacrificed to espresso machines and computer

15

terminals; up on the wall an old photograph of Dame Henrietta Barnett herding sheep across the fields where the Hampstead Garden Suburb now stood, but which had once been an Edwardian interzone).

Then, I had paid no particular attention to Ballard, regarding his works as of a piece with all the other dystopias I hung out in. Possibly I had noticed a certain harder edge, a smoother dovetailing between the commonplace and the fantastic; maybe the wanting seed had been planted. Whatever. But when I *reread* Ballard the seed germinated with nightmarish speed, sending shoots into every portion of my brain. I had been struggling – as every wannabe writer should – with what it was that I could conceivably write. My experience was both threadbare and mundane: the conveyor-belt smoothness of tarmac paths between green privet curtains; dysfunctional family neuroses as regularly patterned as Sanderson's wallpaper; painful experimentation with drugs – teaching myself to shoot up, puncturing my skinny forearms with needles while outside the steel-framed windows pigeons cooburbled. 'The human organism is an atrocity exhibition at which he is an unwilling spectator.'* All this, I knew, was nothing, my mind was a *tabula rasa* sullied with the smears of licked fingertips picking up granules of cocaine and amphetamine sulphate.

Before I'd gone into rehab I'd essayed a few things: a post-apocalyptic novella called 'The Caring Ones', in which the ton of diamorphine that was allegedly kept in the Mass Disaster Room of the Royal Free Hospital became the cynosure of all power struggles between the pain-ravaged survivors of the bomb. I still have the MS somewhere – but that says more about my obsessive need to accumulate paper than anything else, for it was crap. Utter crap. There were also a handful of comic vignettes, and reams of self-indulgent diarising of the kind that no self-respecting crafter of fiction should ever permit. I had ideas, certainly, but no authenticity with which to anchor them.

Ballard showed the way: the fiction of the twenty-first century, the fiction that would *matter*, was there on the Isle of Grain, there in the interzones, there in the psyches of all of us who appreciated the three-mile sinuous chicane of the Westway flyover, there in our numbed responses to those superfluities of space and time, that, together with our own narcissistic subjectivity, constituted the very essence of what Marc Augé has termed, 'supermodernity'. That Ballard had got there first – and got there farthest – was only testimony to his genius. He was one of that small

---

16 * J. G. Ballard, *The Atrocity Exhibition* (1970).

coterie of artists who, unafraid of the consequences, had been prepared to turn their minds over to the dæmons of creation to make of them what they would. Acutely conscious that in the post-lapsarian world that followed the Holocaust and Hiroshima, no value would escape re-evaluation, Ballard had turned his back on the cosy sentimentalities of so-called naturalistic fiction, its immersion in the he-said, she-said, we-watched of inter-personality. No longer, he averred, could the novelist – like an origami deity – fix fate by folding the page.

Six years later, in Shepperton, I was a published writer – and what was far better, Ballard had read my stuff and approved. I switched on the tape recorder and we talked for a couple of hours,* talked easily, ranging freely across the fictional terrain where our estates marched. There were anecdotes that Jim told, the matter of which was not unexpected: the genuine paranoia of William Burroughs, whom he had known fairly well in the 1970s; the continuing capacity of his cloistered life to confound visitors; the whisky . . . but overall it was a conversation about writing, and the worlds that writing actualised, and a conversation about the world, and the writings that it provoked.

The shadows crept across the pocket-handkerchief lawn; if, at the outset, I had been thinking of Jim as a putative parent, when it was time for me to go I was having difficulty not regarding him as a friend. I was heading back to town, to Soho, to meet up with Damien Hirst and his coterie. ('He's a really a novelist,' Jim had said. 'Who writes very short books.') There would be a lot of drinking, a lot of cocaine, a headlong fall into a dark night of shebeens and spielers. Did he…? I ventured to Jim . . . ever go out much? Would it be possible for us to meet up again?

And here, perhaps, my memory lets me down, because what I *think* Ballard said in reply was one of the most pithily instructive lessons about life and literature that I've ever been given. True, it was a little late for me to be learning this – but then, no one had ever offered to teach me before. No, he said, he didn't go out much – and besides, there was probably too great a disparity in our ages for us to find much common social ground; moreover, writers knowing one another *in the flesh* was almost entirely beside the point: the true communion existed in the texts, and we had that with each other already.

Having placed myself so overtly as a disciple, and then – quite uncharacteristically – to have risked the rebuff, I was surprised by how well I took it. As I walked

---

* The transcription was published in my first collection of journalism, *Junk Mail* (Bloomsbury, 1995).

back to the station it occurred to me that this was because what Ballard had said, he meant, and that furthermore: it was true. There could be no greater meeting of minds than the one we had already experienced amid the twisted hulks of cars abandoned en route to the terminal beach; even sexually, with his easy acceptance – on the page – of the homoerotic I had assessed the heft of his body, apprehended the geometry of his genitals. If Ballard felt the same way about me – even a small part of it – then it remained a far more mutual relationship than any I had ever contracted for through the mere accident of propinquity.

And so I took him at his word, and kept away. A year or so later, when I heard that David Cronenberg was about to film Ballard's *Crash*, I did get in touch. In the novel, the car crash cult's field of operations was the badlands in the purlieus of Heathrow Airport, the scrublands of Hillingdon and Hayes, the cavernous warehouses and hangars of its Perimeter Road, the reservoir-cratered moonscape of Staines and Shepperton itself – where Ballard's alter ego, 'Jim', also lives. To transpose this to Toronto would be a dreadful solecism.

I got Jim on the phone: 'No, no,' he barked in his genial RAF-officer tones. 'You don't get it at all. The whole point of *Crash* is that it could take place anywhere in the urbanised world. I absolutely *relish* the idea of Cronenberg filming in Toronto, it's the perfect location – so anonymous, so dreary.'

I stayed away from Shepperton, writing only the occasional note, or sending a book I'd published, or a bottle of Scotch I thought he might like. When my third child was born Jim sent me a letter: 'Now they outnumber you!' But of course, ever since his wife's death in 1964, he himself had been completely outnumbered. Eventually, in 2006, I returned, with the pretext of another interview. This time I came on a folding bicycle and pedalled my way down the suburban street, but otherwise everything remained the same: the somnolent semi, with the yucca in the front window now completely overgrown, a triffid that had usurped the household and now perhaps demanded its own troublesome cups of tea.

I had already heard rumours that Jim was ill, but he seemed perfectly hale – intrigued by my folding bicycle, and altogether welcoming. Once we were seated at the table in the front room he expostulated: 'Why don't you ever come to see me!' And the last twelve years fell away like multicoloured fish scales; I almost blurted out: 'But you told me . . . !' then didn't, instead we talked as before, yet this time – or so it seemed to me – with an easier intimacy: time does this to human lives, evening them up, so that in due course the jejeune disciple becomes the well-worn near-contemporary. Jim talked of his time in the internment camp in Shanghai, and with great frankness of the horrors he had witnessed as a child. The novel that was about to be published, *Kingdom Come*, was in some ways a retread of preoccupations he had explored in his writing going all the way back to *High Rise* (1975) – material sufficiency as a prelude to dreadful ennui, violence as an antidote to boredom, *enfin* the revolt of the bourgeoisie – but from the way he discussed his past I now realise that Jim must already have been engaged on the memoir *Miracles of Life*.

Two or three dinners in Shepherd's Bush followed. We ate either at the Brackenbury or Esarn Kheaw, a northern Thai restaurant. These were quietly sociable affairs – Jim, Claire, my wife Deborah Orr and I. The talk was of current events, families, the patchwork of cultural interests to be expected of such representative types: writers, editors, journalists. In many ways the meetings were antithetical to the fierce communion I had experienced with Jim's psyche in the pages of his books. I had started out, in the 1970s, following him along a cramped and dangerous tunnel when he was unquestionably in the avant garde, hacking away at the rage-resistant fabric of society, inching his way forward into conceptual space; now we sat opposite one another at a candlelit table and chatted about the London Congestion Charge. I liked both modalities equally well.

Jim had never made any secret of his diagnosis with terminal prostate cancer – he had been open in the press and frank in person. But there was, I felt, a strange disconnection between his seeming acceptance of his own death, and his manner, which suggested that the valediction itself could be an eternity. First, the memoir, and now there was a second book of leave-taking in the pipeline, a series of discourses with his oncologist, Jonathan Waxman. I took this stoicism as in line with a life that in some respects had been lived backwards: the tight bomb-pattern of *thanatos* falling in the first three decades, the subsequent ones more and more vivified; and contrasted it with my own overweening neurosis, the mewling all morning over a hangnail, the adolescent hysteria that popped up to accompany the pubescent spots that still erupted on my middle-aged face.

So, suffused with all this, I decided to walk to The World, the collection of artificial islands scooped out of the Arabian Sea, and bulldozed into an approximation of the world's landmasses. This was only the latest of the property developments in Dubai that had transmogrified the once sleepy Trucial Coast into a child's drawing of paradise, visible only using Google Earth: the sandy coastline a crude foreground; the concrete trunk and fronds of the Palm Jumeirah an equally botched representation, set against a shallow sea-for-sky; The World itself, plonked down on the wrinkled and glaucous page with no concern for the conventions of perspective or pictorial space, while ranged around it were the crude spirals and lumpy galaxies of the Universe (proposed). To the left was the Palm Jebel Ali (under construction), while to the right was the Palm Deira (entirely debatable land).

En route to The World, stomping along the Sheik Zayed Road from the airport, I would stop off at another figuration, the Burj Dubai, putatively the world's tallest building – already it had motored past the Sears Tower to have the greatest number of habitable floors of any building: 160. The Burj had surpassed the world's loftiest freestanding structure – the CN Tower (1,815 feet) – and pushed above the world's highest structure of all – the KVLY-TV mast (2,065 feet) – to waver in the desert sky, a concrete and steel stamen, its triple-lobed core an embodiment of Islamic architectural practices, being – or so we were assured – based on an abstraction of the petals of the flower *Hymenocallis*.

'Later, as he sat on his balcony eating the dog, Dr Robert Laing reflected on the unusual events that had taken place within this huge apartment building during the previous three months.' The opening lines of *High Rise* set the bar appropriately high for fictional prognostication, written as they were almost a decade before the foundations for Canary Wharf, London's tallest building, were dug, yet situating Ballard's tower block, unerringly, in the abandoned docklands of the Isle of Dogs. So, I would walk from the writer's house in Shepperton towards this terrifying gnomon, the cast shadow of which told us only that our time was up. I would trudge through the raw materials of his fictive process, among the shopping centres and the reservoirs, crossing the motorways and skirting the gravel pits; then, at Heathrow's Terminal 5, my body would have carried me into the cockpit of the High Modernism to which my *maître* had always had such a profound ambivalence.

SUBURBAN ODYSSEY

Ralph STEADman 2009

It seemed only meet, this ingurgitation of the organic by the machined; next, a wrench skywards – Ballard, an air force-trained pilot himself, had described with unaffected joy, in *The Kindness of Women*, the exhilaration of flight, while for me the 50,000 pounds of forward thrust, I knew, would only push me back down into ennui. But then there would be the landfall, the airport smack-bang in downtown Dubai, and while there would be the tedium of Costa Coffee – its franchise stretched to gird the earth – once I stepped from the terminal I'd be confronted with all the hazardous futility involved in pitting a pedestrian against the taut and expanding surface of the biggest property bubble the world has ever seen . . . except that it had popped. The word was that the multi-storey car parks at Dubai airport were full of Mercedes and BMWs abandoned by fleeing European expatriates, desperately evading debt – an imprisoning offence in this banjaxed principality.\*

The Dubai boom, which had seen this Lilliputian country push up Brobdingnagian skyscrapers with Promethean alacrity, had never been anything save the most glaring example of Guy Debord's society of the spectacle: the mounding then patty-cake-shaping of capital itself into an image – or an idol. The money had come from the Gulf – oily lucre, piped across the sands – or else from Russian mafia; or from Indian, Chinese and Japanese organised crime. Then again, investment had zapped electronically across the Atlantic after the terrorist attacks of September 11th, 2001; so that as two skyscrapers crashed into the dust, another forest of them – irrigated by liquidity – arose on the obverse of 'the world'. No, there was no reason for all this office space and all these luxury apartments on the fringes of the great desert of Arabia's Empty Quarter, none at all – looked at one way Dubai City was only a buy-to-let scheme for oil bunce and capital flight; drug, gun and whoring money; a great dung heap of pelf that, naturally, attracted plenty of flies – 100,000 from the United Kingdom alone.

They were the lucky ones – they had wings. The Indian and Korean civil engineers could also, one hoped, flit away if they had to. But then there were the ants – the Pakistanis, Baluchis and Bangladeshis who laboured on the construction sites, hacked the cabs and cleaned the luxury apartments; the Ethiopians and Sudanese who plucked the litter from the sidewalks, and the Filipino 'maids' who scrubbed European, American and Arab shit from the toilet bowls. They had been brought

---

\*   Cars were not merely abandoned. Johann Hari, for his excellent exposé of post-boom Dubai (*Independent*, 9 April 2009), actually interviewed an expatriate British woman who, mired in debt, was living in her Land Rover.

SHEIKS CANT DO PERSPECTIVE FOR TOFFEE!

PATTY-CAKE MIRAGE with U'K FLIES —

here, many by unscrupulous gang masters, who deducted their living expenses at source and confiscated their passports. There had been labour unrest – but only the most high-profile abuses had been tidied away. Now, in the razor-wire-wreathed, concrete blockhouses of Ajman and Sonapur, there were thousands of migrant workers stranded with no work. 'The entrenched' they were called: small brown men, eking out their meagre lives with tiny tan snacks – vegetable pakora costing a single dhiram. Unable to go home, unable to send any money home – their sole reason for being in Dubai – they squatted in the alleys between the blocks, the sands of time pitting their faces . . . As it was so it is: after all, slavery – especially of Africans – was an Arabian institution that endured well into the last century. Meanwhile, the discarded prostitutes – so many anthropoid tissues – were crumpled up, packed into aircraft, and flown elsewhere in the world to sop up more patriarchal jism.

Looked at another way, this instant metropolis was at once a Petit Trianon and a Potemkin village. Presumably Sheikh Mohammed bin Rashid Al Maktoum, and his tiny brigade of native Emiratis – a mere eighth of the Emirate's 1.65 million inhabitants – had a psychological need to play at being urbanites, and so escape the trans-generational neurosis of their famously austere forefathers. To flee, en bloc, to Paris or London or Los Angeles, and remain there in perpetuity, would be unthinkable, so instead they had built a Wendy conurbation for themselves, one they could drive through in their Hummers, on the way to the mall with the ski run in it, or the refrigerated beach, or to play with horses and lanner falcons in what remained of the desert. Gazing upon the cladding of the skyscrapers, perhaps they half-convinced themselves that within there were armies of purposeful bureaucrats, feisty entrepreneurs and creative professionals. To reverse the hoary adage, maybe for the Sheikh and his countrymen, there *were* no migrant workers, only fellow citizens yet to be granted civil rights. Or so I imagined – the alternative, that they *desired* this Sparta of the mind, where helots laid down their lives to wrest Tiger Woods Dubai from the desert, was too awful to contemplate.

Unfortunately, while the thought of the walk to The World galvanised my imagination, and I had gone so far as to arrange the practicalities: the flights, the hotels, the trip out to the archipelago with a complaisant – and complacent – PR, an interview with one of the architectural team piling up the Burj Dubai, yet still I found myself unable to do the reading. I ought – I thought – to steep myself in *Arabia Deserta* and *The Seven Pillars of Wisdom*; I should have a mental picture of where the historical horizon lay, lest I be deceived by the mirages and dust devils of Sheikh Mo's fantasia on the theme of urbanisation. Instead, as the coldest winter for a decade came to an end, I found myself, in bed, comfort reading, yet again, Shackleton's account of his 1908–9 attempt on the South Pole: '. . . we cannot get on South and we simply lie here shivering. We must do something more to the South even though the food is going and we weaken lying in the cold for . . . even the drift is finding its way into our bags which . . . are wet and damp enough as it is.'

A century on, it was perfectly dry and warm under my duvet, while the only thing finding its way in was a drift of biscuit crumbs. Usually this exercise in time-travelling *Schadenfreude* does it for me; inducing more and more repose as I contemplate the suffering of yore: men torturing themselves to reach a location that, by reason of their obsession alone, has become nothing but an abstraction. My own home becomes more and more *gemütlich* as I dwell on the remote desolation of the Burberry-clad explorers, pinned down in their tent by the blizzards on the Antarctic ice cap. Not this time. Abed in south London, the radio on, listening to the news of the ceaseless electronic blizzard that was winnowing out the London Stock Exchange – billions of pounds blown into a howling void – it occurred to me that my own projected walk was nothing but a grotesque diminuendo of Shackletonian endeavour.

Like Shacks, dragging his sleighs across the crevasses and sastrugi, I was eschewing all the proven means of efficient travel over these concrete and bitumen wastes, in favour of man-hauling; and like Shacks, I was attempting to connect a Romantic myth to a geographic location. For him and his fellow Imperialist explorers, it was the linkage between individual courage and the frontiers of the known world, while for me it was the yoking of individual perversity to the under-imagined interzones of a world in which the map has taken precedence over the territory it describes – except that the maps were barely adequate when it came to Dubai.

When Wilfred Thesiger had crossed the Empty Quarter of Arabia in 1947 – a journey of Shackletonian hardship that ended with a leisurely sojourn on the Trucial Coast, and hawking expeditions with Sheikh Mo's granddad – the great chains of dunes, the quicksands and the wadis had never been accurately surveyed. Thesiger did the job himself, with a compass and theodolite, while quizzing his Bedouin companions, who, he was amused to note, had difficulty in relating the rudimentary map he made to their territory, unless it was held in the correct orien-

MONEY BLIZZARD

tation. A mere sixty years later, the remaining hinterland of Dubai, on the fringes of the Empty Quarter, was once again unmapped, except on a scale of 1:400,000, woefully inadequate for someone proceeding at 3 mph.

There were maps of Dubai City at a more apprehensible scale, although these were aspirational rather than achieved depictions – for on the page, the purlieus of the city were ringed with massive figures, crude geometric shapes inscribed on the bare desert, the Nazca lines of the construction gods. The legends read: 'Golf City (U/C)', 'Al Maktoum International Airport (U/C)', 'Extreme Sports World (U/C)', and 'Dubai Heritage Vision (U/C)', while not forgetting Tiger Woods Dubai, which was also under construction. This looked forbidding enough, but the built-up area was hardly more inviting, sliced up as it was into development areas by the Sheikh and his cronies – a complex web of property combines, at the very nexus of which, with a 99.67 per cent stake in Dubai Holdings, squatted the *soi-disant* 'constitutional monarch'. The diagrammatic outlines of Al Quoz Industrial Area 3 and Emirates Hills 2 were connected to each other by freeways alone. From the map I could tell that this was the world of Ballard's novels and stories: modular and introverted zones, where social relations had been defined by a CAD-CAM program, and pedestrianism was a leisure activity inseparable from retail opportunities.

To walk, as I intended to do, from the airport clear across the city to the Palm Jumeirah, via the Burj Dubai development, would be tough enough, but after I had taken the boat trip to The World, my intention was to head due south, out into the desert, and using my body as the measure of all things, unstitch the fabric of time itself, tearing away the decades until the land was once more unadorned – or, would I be privileged with a glimpse of the future, when the oil was all gone, and the decaying skyscrapers were vast and trunkless stumps, while the trenches gouged in the *bled* could only be read from orbit: My name is Tiger Woods, look upon my shattered Golf World and . . . despair.

Whichever. The fact of the matter was that I could only roughly locate Bab Al Shams – a costly 'desert resort' hotel that I had booked myself into – using Google Earth and the large-scale map, while the eighteen miles between it and the edge of Dubai City, at Jumeirah Village South (U/C), remained just as much of a terra incognita as they had been to Thesiger, when he and his Rashid companions rode their camels up the coast from Abu Dhabi. It was a humbling testimony to how in thrall I was to the graphical world that this teensy wilderness should so bedevil me. Night after night I sat in my writing room poring over the computer screen and the dodgy maps, futilely attempting to marry them together, and so discover

27

what lay in store. Even in early March the temperatures in the desert could reach the 100s; to get lost out there would be no joke. I was reduced to zooming in on the satellite image as far as I could and then 'walking' the route, while making the assumption that the orientation on the screen was accurate, for that of the maps – given their crudity – seemed altogether dubious. In the final analysis, I would have to rely, just as Thesiger had, on dead reckoning with a compass. *Plus-ça-fucking-change*. 'A hundred-foot-long panel that seemed to represent a section of a sand dune. Looking at it more closely Dr Nathan realized that in fact it was an immensely magnified portion of the skin over the iliac crest.'[*]

I left the house at a sunny noontime in early March and proceeded to Vauxhall Station past the Portuguese cafés and marginally distinguishable convenience stores of the South Lambeth Road. Up ahead were the gull's wing penthouses of St George's Wharf at Vauxhall Cross, a comprehensive uglification that even after a decade remained (U/C). The walk to The World already felt freighted with too much baggage – although I, as ever, travelled excessively light. Moreover, the purity of my trek had been compromised: the PR at Nakheel, The World's developers, had emailed me a couple of days previously: the Prophet's birthday – a curiously moveable feast, it seemed – had been switched to the Sunday, and I would be unable to go out to the archipelago that day. So, instead, I was walking to the desert resort, and would have to walk back to The World on the Monday.

There was this disappointment, and there was also the melancholia – wasn't this a valedictory walk, and an *hommage*, of sorts? I had spoken to Jim a couple of times on the phone in the preceding weeks, and while he sounded altogether present, there were definable limits to anyone's ability to remain in two places at once: standing on the platform, while also waving from the train that pulls away. In his postcards, which were usually depictions of his own Delvaux paintings, or other Surrealist works, Jim had maintained, fully intact, his gimlet eye. Chemotherapy was, he wrote, 'like continually eating bad oysters', while morphine rendered him 'unable to write a letter to my accountant of the most matter-of-fact kind'. And so, for as long as he could, he had abjured the stuff.

I thought it not without significance that in his communications Jim's most frequent term of approbation was 'lucid', and although, as someone who'd been addicted to opiates, on and off, for over two decades, I had come to lucidity – and correspondence with accountants – a little late in life, I now prized it quite as

[*]  J. G. Ballard, *The Atrocity Exhibition*, (1970).

fiercely as he. The lucidity required to focus on the very particular kind of dust that, regardless of the passage of time, and the reallocation of rail franchises, always seems to fur the upholstery of British train seats. The lucidity required to scrutinise the headlines on the discarded free newspapers that lay about the carriage: £150 BILLION: THE LAST THROW OF THE DICE; this, a reference to the government's plan for 'quantitative easing', an oddly scatological-sounding euphemism for printing money: the economy was chronically constipated; Britannia sat, contorted on the commode. The lucidity necessary to allow the train of thought to clack across the synaptic points: opiates . . . constipation . . . Thesiger's *Arabian Sands*, in which he described a ritual performed on one of his companions who was so afflicted: 'He lay on the ground while a dozen of his friends knelt round him in a circle chanting . . . which got faster and faster as the participants got more and more excited. At intervals one of the singers would lean forward and take up a mouthful of flesh from Mussallim's stomach, making a curious bubbling noise as he did so. Mussallim's bowels were loosened soon after this.'

It might well be – it occurred to me as the Shepperton train clattered through Wimbledon – that this was the real reason for my walk to the Empty Quarter; perhaps only there, in complete isolation, delivered from the tense typing that was my daily weal, would I manage a truly satisfying shit.

Melancholia – an excess of humours. The previous evening, in Bath, I'd had dinner with the philosopher John Gray, at a buffet restaurant called The Real China in a small shopping mall. John, a friend of Jim Ballard's, had been enthusiastic about the walk to The World: 'Dubai will be the perfect place from which to observe the collapse of the capitalist system!' he exclaimed over chicken in black bean sauce. We spoke of Ballard's story cycle *Vermillion Sands*; while we could recall the content – washed-up roués and fading actresses, artists of the floating world grounded in a derelict desert resort – we couldn't locate where these dreamy interactions took place. John spoke of his own visit to the Gulf, flown in by an international consortium in his capacity as a rental futurologist: 'I arrived during Ramadan and there was nothing, it seemed, to eat. They put me up in a massive antiseptic hotel. Eventually, somewhere like the 35th floor, I found an entire reconstruction of a Watney's pub, circa 1975, complete with pudgy and miserable British expats, sitting around watching darts on a satellite television – it was hell on earth.'

We discussed where we might retreat to if the four horsemen took a generous dump on southern England. I floated the idea of Iceland, where the worst had already happened, and the populace were accustomed to hardy self-sufficiency –

Bedouin pitched up on a lava field – but John favoured middle America: 'There are towns there, in places like Virginia, that are completely safe – no one even locks their front door. Of course, they're effectively plantations, colonies in the country they pretend to be a part of.'

Melancholia. In Shepperton I stopped at the newsagent by the station to buy a disposable lighter. The headline in the Surrey Advertiser read: 'TAKE THAT! Did Driver with a Grudge Take it Out on a Speed Camera?' Judging by the photo of the camera in question, battered out of all recognition, the answer could only be affirmative – out here in the 'burbs stirred the violence born of affluence that Ballard had hymned since the 1960s, its object the monocular stare of the surveillance society. Jim's road was exactly the same, the pampas grass and the bungalows, the Edwardian solidity of The Laurels, 1911, and the metallic silvery bulk of the writer's Ford Granada, slumped on the adverse camber of his drive. All was as before, with only the slow-exploding fractals of Jim's mutant yucca to indicate the passing of the years.

At the far end, the well-parsed sentence of Jim's road was terminated by the full stop of a pub; beyond, a boggily inarticulate meadow edged by the muddy stream of the River Ash, and beyond that a golf course. A footbridge – perfect in its way, a curlicue of ferro-concrete, a calligraphic embellishment on the text – led me up and over the M3 motorway. On the far side I refused the road and plunged into an interzone. I lunged between stands of saplings and played Twister with tangles of brambles. All this negligence had been encouraged, between the motorway and a flooded gravel pit, to frustrate exactly my sort of passage. Deep in, hemmed on all sides, struggling to remove the thorns ripping my shins, the sunlight filtering through the undergrowth, the traffic swishing on the far side of the crash barrier, I felt the melancholia shift a little, then scuttle sideways into simple sadness.

It never failed me, this: the oblique step into spaces that interrogated the prescribed folkways – why are you going so fast? Why from A to B? Why not L to F? – laying bare the hollowness of their Manifest Destiny. A slop across a ditch, sunlight on a tawny field, Canada and Brent geese trying it on in the furrows, quiffs of alder against deep blue water, a couplet of semis outlined by the green glacis of the Queen Mary reservoir – behind it were 200 million gallons of water rising sixty feet above the flatlands, and capped by a three-kilometre-square meniscus. I scaled a fence, then a second and wandered up a track to stare out across this inland sea; Gulf+Western clouds streamed overhead. I rummaged my psyche for hidden profundities – was the juxtaposition of all this fresh water and the desert ahead prefigured by the excesses and depletions of Jim's prescient environmental disaster novels – *The Drowned World*, *The Drought*, *The Wind from Nowhere*?

All that afternoon I wandered on, from the reservoir to Shepperton Studios where, for a while, I watched a rehearsal of a swordfight – chivalry in jeans and trainers. Then to Laleham, where I joined the Thames towpath, and accelerated upstream, striding past interwar villas and apartment blocks, rounding the long bend at Penton Hook, then loping into Staines, a surpassingly brutal town centre, dominated by the glassy nullity of the BUPA head office – you would need private health insurance to *survive* in this place, to sally confidently into the bastion of its civic bollix, dominated by the Elmsleigh Centre, a shopping mall not unlike the one envisioned by Ballard in *Kingdom Come*: 'Illuminated arrays glowed through the night, like the perimeter lights of a colony of prison camps, a new gulag of penal settlements where the forced labour was shopping and spending . . .'

Mushroom and Emmental flat bread, a china basin of Earl Grey tea. I sat up above River Island, Timpson and La Senza in a branch of Costa Coffee, feeling my ankles fizz with nettle stings and thorn scratches. Around me the Staines lasses chattered amiably: exposed midriffs and nose studs, coordinated pink tracksuits and pink iPods. Yet units were vacant in the mall below, and not for some years had things – qua things – seemed quite so hollow; it was only people's acquisitiveness that had given them any solidity, now all the black boxes in Dixon's were as vacuous as balloons; if you shook them you would hear the rattle of that little dried pea, the globe.

Union flags flopped on the flagpoles in front of the houses along the quiet roads that drew me out of town. When I reached the tumulus of the George VI Reservoir, the signs warning DEEP WATER were high above my head, up there with the life preservers. The fence posts – each a savage little trident – marched away into the distance; at a place called – aptly enough – 'Bone Head', I detoured across Staines Moor. Sitting out there, smoking, beside the crack willows edging the Colne River, in among wavering head-height reeds, I watched as the missiles shot over the green ramparts from Heathrow were silvered in the rays of the setting sun. It struck me that the logical extension of Jim's trope was that globalisation itself was a form of siege warfare – one fought with human ordinance.

This damp clout of discarded land – the moor, a soggy farm, the gates to its fields festooned with fading tape: 'Foot and Mouth Disease KEEP OUT' – was a seabed across which fled a tiny tribe of a half a Jew, while to the east and the west the inland seas had, over the decades, been so long immured that sheep grazed on their complacent bulges. This, I thought, can all change; then I walked on, leaving my map behind.

Toiling up the Perimeter Road with the dusk and sadness synched, the jewel box of T5 sparkled behind the dull moiré of security fencing. From this vantage, on the south-western side of the airport, the view was unobstructed all the way to Hatton: three miles of grassland, a pocket prairie left wild in the heart of England. Another runway might be built – or not; the siege would continue – or be lifted. It hardly mattered, the blades would continue to comb the wind, T5 would hum and pulse, an open secret of a military installation, purpose-built to facilitate a close encounter – with ourselves.

From the waiting area at the gate for my flight, where fractious parents rounded up their toddlers again, and again, I phoned Claire and she put Jim on the line. I told him about the walk from Shepperton to Heathrow, the inversion of water and land, the submarine bungalows and the inundated landfills along the Laleham Road. He was encouraging – 'I am, you know, a great fan of your work . . .' and then, abruptly, gone. 'Send us a postcard,' Claire said. 'We love postcards.' And then she was gone also, and the sadness thickened and thickened, until it curdled into melancholy – then I was alone with it, an affluent middle-aged orphan, rounded up again and again, then hustled into an airline seat.

OBLIGATORY
IN-FLIGHT
SCRIBBLE.

The diminutive girl-woman who sat beside me on the way to Dubai read her book, a historical detective story by someone I knew – vaguely, it's a small and papery world – or else she slept, as snug as a kitten in its basket. I read about the ascent of the bin Laden family to become the concrete-pourers by appointment to the House of Saud. It was a fascinating tale: the hegira of Mohammed bin Laden, the founder of the dynasty from the stony towers and rocky ravines of the Yemen to the foetid port of Jeddah, where the ancient buildings were stuck together with a mucilage of crushed coral; his death, three decades later, in a light aircraft accident on a visit to one of his desert construction sites. His son and heir Salem's death, twenty years after that, footling around in a microlight in Texas – the family's destiny was all about this: the juxtaposition of the airy and the weighty, stratospheric dreams and concrete realities. While Salem's half-brother and successor, Bakr, was jetting around the world in the late 1990s, fixing up the deals that would transform the Great Mosque at Mecca into a theme park, 'Muslimworld', his half-brother Osama squatted in the Sudan. Seen one way, Osama was planning the shaming of the *umma*, by means of a spectacular that would alert them to the profanation of the holy places; an alternative view was that he was pitching – albeit in a convoluted fashion – for a construction contract. The jihad, the War on Terror – these were the boardroom struggles of a family firm – by proxy.

I read, ate too much, asked the stewardess for more chocolate, and eventually slept fitfully – farting under my thin blanket; it felt as if, far from digesting, the food was reconstituting itself into small, hard, foil-lidded oblong trays. At high-speed dawn, the young woman on the far side of the cabin got up, went to the toilet, and emerged a half hour later perfectly groomed and changed into a sun dress. My own girl-woman stirred as the plane began its descent, bumping high above the grey-whale humps of the Omani mountains. Was she enjoying the book? I asked. 'No,' she sighed prettily. 'It jumps about too much.' Narrative instability bothered her mightily, but she was perfectly at ease with the disarticulation of space/time: she'd been to Dubai 'three or four times', it was, she thought, 'a good place for a weekend'.

To prolong the conversation – leaning across her tiny lap, the smog-wreathed reef of the city rearing up from the sea – I asked her if she'd ever taken a walk in Dubai. She thought for a while then answered carefully, 'To be honest, I think the longest walk I've ever taken was when I went on a bus tour.' I looked past her to the street plan below, as exposed as micro-circuitry, and tried to see if there were sidewalks.

Sheikh Mo, who, like his bin Laden namesake in Saudi Arabia, likes to pitch up at construction sites unannounced – such charming informality – will nonetheless brook no opposition to his benignity: websites critical of his regime are blocked in the Emirate, as are pornographic ones. This sets up the following bizarre antimony: in Dubai City you can fuck whores – if you have the money – and get righteously fucked over, while sexual thought crimes – and homosexuality, natch – remain firmly on the statute book. Actually, prostitution is technically illegal as well, not that that's ever stopped those who have the money from knocking back vodka shots in the lobby of the Moscow Hotel, before heading upstairs with a whore. Moreover, woe betide you if you so much as touch down in Dubai with a micro-gram of dope balled in the lint at the bottom of your pocket. This was not the place to make landfall – as I had, in Kirkwall Airport, in January 1994 – with an ounce of hash stuck in your sock.

I had such impure thoughts about the regime, and although clean as a whistle for a decade now, there were years before when my body had functioned – in relation to drugs – much as a bivalve's does to brine, so I approached the spotless white headdresses at the immigration desk with some trepidation – only to be franked unceremoniously in: of as little substance as a ghost, or a small mirage of foreign currency. So it went on: caffeinated and dosed with nicotine, I walked up the exit ramp unchallenged, past the multi-storey car parks chock-full of abandoned Mercs, and into a desert city where I was, to all intents and purposes, invisible.

I strode along the well-appointed sidewalk of the Airport Road, and crossed over a footbridge furnished with air conditioning and escalators – what was this, a triumphal arch for the pedestrian? With such infrastructure, this walk – I foolishly imagined – was going to be a *doddle*. At the junction with Sheikh Rashid Road, Sheikh Mo looked down on me from a giant billboard fixed to the side of a building that had all the architectural merit – and instant obsolescence – of a CD tower. In London I am often tormented by the distortions in scale provoked by postmodernism: a skyline of executive desk toys, set down higgledy-piggledy by some middle-management deity, but Dubai makes the most fatuous agglomerations of European office space seem like venerable cathedral cities, dense with civic history, profoundly lived in.

I set off towards the colossal bulk of the Dubai City Centre mall, judging from my street map that I might work my way down behind it to the creek where there were dhow wharfs, and so enjoy some human scale in among these giant paperclip pots and steely note holders. No dice – there was no way to cross the road, which was six lanes complete with an elevated section U/C – so I beat a retreat. Besides, I was still worrying about my journey without maps. In a last attempt before I left I had ordered a Dubai off-road map that boasted it was one of 'the largest-scale maps available for the UAE'. It turned out to be a laminated satellite photograph that its purchaser could 'use with your GPS to navigate your way in the outback, and back out again!'

Ha-fucking-ha. The map was sponsored by Hummer, of course, and what was worse my one – Number 2 – didn't even cover the desert I wanted to walk across; for that I required Number 5. The guidebook said there was a good bookshop in the Deira City Centre mall – I owed it to my anxiety to at least try and find the right map. As I made my way back a queer fact about Dubai began to impinge on me – to get anywhere on foot you had to dodge across traffic streams, and cut

A WELCOME SITE...!

through construction sites, but no matter how abandoned my transits, or how close I strayed to earthmoving equipment – and even arc-welding – no one paid me the slightest attention. It took a few hours of this invisibility for me to fully comprehend its reason. I saw plenty of pedestrians on my walk to The World, but without exception they all had black or brown skins – the only whites I noticed on foot were hopping about in the immediate surroundings of buildings. There was this aspect to the racial divide, and there was also a more chilling *omertà*: if I was white, I must have legitimate business, and just as the guest workers would only speak if spoken to, so, clearly, it was forbidden for them to address me.

It was mid-morning, and the temperature outside was already in the mid-80s, but inside the mall the commerce was chilly. I spoke to Slavs in shops full of stylishly distressed denim, and Indians tending displays of Swiss watches, but no one knew anything about a bookshop. Finally, completely exasperated, I collared a native: he was graceful enough – no, the bookshop had shut down. There was one in the Dubai City mall – or else, there was, he thought, a book section in Spinney's the supermarket. In a scant hour I had gone from triumph to defeat – to backtrack to the other mall would cost me time I could ill afford if I was to make my destination for the night, the Holiday Inn Express in Knowledge City. I found myself squatting in Spinney's, while around me the polyglot crowd bought toilet paper, and futilely examining the maps on offer, exactly the same ones that had been available in London – examining them with neurotic intent, as if they might unfold to reveal a hidden flap, upon which this dilemma was described: the little-hellishness of using out-of-date guidebooks to try and track down inadequate maps. For a few craven moments as I passed back through the mall and stared at the astigmatism of screens in an electronics store, I even considered buying a handheld GPS.

Then I got a grip on myself and struck out for the creek, where I took a waterbus across to the far side. The Burj Dubai wavered to the south-east, a veridical needle in a smogstack, while along the creek itself stood brushed-steel and smoked-glass façades, each with its own surtitle, singing out loud HSBC or ROLEX. The little water taxis cutting across our wake were freighted with Asian *gastarbeiter*, and the hulking dhows anchored to the quays at least had the virtue of looking well-used, piled up above the gunnels with stuff – bales of cloth, building materials, washing machines.

SAND AND CEMENT

The far bank was cluttered with older buildings – I could even make out a few with the wind towers Thesiger would've seen in the 1940s – and the cloth souk I passed through on disembarking had the bustling crowds and haggling huddles of a personalised space. Some called Dubai 'the finest city in India' – but India is inseparable from its smell, and as I made my way through the Bur Dubai and Al Raffa districts, then out along the Al Mankhool Road towards the residential area of Satwa, the atmosphere was perfumed only with petrol fumes, charcoal and fat frying.

I cursed myself for a fool, labouring along the pavement, past air-conditioned bus shelters. This time the airport walk hadn't worked; on previous journeys – from my house to New York, Los Angeles and even Zurich – the mediation of distance by legs alone, with only the dull pause of an airline seat interpolated, had pulled these landmasses into crushing proximity: it felt as if I had walked all the way, so, *ipso facto*, Hayes, Middlesex, Jamaica, Long Island and the orderly little 'burb of Oerlikon all sprawled together, overlooked not only by the wooded bulk of the Zurichberg, but the Baldwin Hills as well.

It struck me that it must have been because I had walked from Jim Ballard's house in Shepperton rather than my own, that the desired spatial consummation had not been achieved; moreover, if I had taken the time to go through the outer London and south Asian district of Southall – the logical parallel to Satwa – then I'd be more at home in this world; as it was I felt tired, alienated and began to doubt the validity of my quest: what was the point of these rambles anyway? They told me nothing that I didn't know already, or, rather, my method imposed on the raw data of experience a prefabricated narrative: everywhere was the same; everyone was forced to follow the same road/rail/flight path, only I had escaped the man/machine matrix to saunter, barefoot, along the median strip.

But wasn't the truth that I was just as determined? Moreover, in eschewing any ground transport, my view of these alien lands was grossly circumscribed, while my ambitious mileages meant that I had no time to stop and stare – let alone sit down in a shisha café and chew the fat with the locals.

In the East, man wants but rest and shade: upon the banks of a bubbling stream or under the cool shelter of a perfumed tree, he is perfectly happy, smoking a pipe or sipping a cup of coffee, or drinking a glass of sherbet, but above all things deranging body and mind as little as possible, the displeasures of memory, and the vanity of thought being the most unpleasant interruptions to his *Kayf*.*

---

* Richard Burton, *Personal Narrative of a Pilgrimage to Al-Madinah and Meccah,* (1855).

Instead, driven full speed ahead by my ambulatory engine, I sat inside the hot, rubbery compartment of my skull, maddened with frustration, staring out through the windscreen of my own eyes.

These gloomy thoughts dogged the ghost in the machine as he floated on along the road, until the minarets of the Satwa mosque hove into view, and he wafted into the backstreets and settled on Ravi's restaurant for lunch. Wittgenstein observed, 'It doesn't matter what you eat as long as it's always the same thing.' I had taken this as my gastronomic motto – if I couldn't marry Shepperton to Satwa with my feet, then I'd do it with my *teeth*, by biting down on exactly the same fare that I'd eat in any Indian restaurant in London: a couple of kathi kebabs, some chapattis and dhal. I sat munching in Ravi's 'family room', next to a table of women in abayas and niqabs, their hands covered in the red-brown lacy filigree of henna tattoos, as more intimate flesh might be sheathed in diaphanous underwear. A couple of Euro-pundits gassed about the economy on a screen in one corner; while on the wall in front of me a portrait of Sheikh Mo countered my blinkered view with his visionary gaze; next to this a picture showed the great throng of pilgrims circumambulating the Kaaba in Mecca. The *Tawaf* is one of the most sacred rituals of the Hajj, the pilgrims are required to walk seven times anticlockwise around the ancient building, starting at the Black Stone, while on each circuit pointing towards it in lieu of a kiss. The Muslims have it that the black stone was chucked down to earth by God, a fiery way marker showing Adam and Eve where to build an altar so as to get to *Him*.

I meditated on this spatial dimension to Islam: the five-times-daily prostrations towards the Kaaba that laid down a million-barred grid of devotion on the surface of the earth; the great influx and then reflux of the hajjis, their myriad journeys fusing the noumenal and phenomenal. The Black Stone and the Kaaba were there before Mohammed, and shorn of folklore, they were only a politically convenient orientation for this global network of faith – but surely this had a purity, and was perhaps the ultimate psychogeography, for, just as all of Islamic doctrine derives logically from a single proposition: 'There is no God but God and Mohammed is his prophet . . .' so all Muslim ritual derives from this location. And what about me, and my pilgrimage to the 2,000-bar concrete pinnacle of the Burj Dubai? What was I involved in here – a religion of one? I texted Deborah in London: 'I'm fine, but I'll tell you one thing – I'm never doing this again.'

Watch-menders sat cross-legged in hutches. An ad plastered to a wall wheedled, 'Available Bed Space for Filipino Ladies'. I walked along streets of single-storey dwellings – blockhouses for the *Gastarbeiter*; through barred windows I could see some men humped in bunk beds, while others played cricket in the rubble-strewn alleys. Cocks pecked at rubbish piles, the dust of construction hung in the afternoon heat haze, as from behind the tangle of aerials the preposterous skyline of the Downtown Dubai development reared up: a skyscraper shaped like a giant lipstick; another four-square, a castle, complete with towers at each corner; a third with its top forming a handle – like Riyadh's odious Kingdom Tower – that a passing Titan might use to wrench it from its foundations. And there was a fourth, its upper storeys corbelled into the neck of a cobra; and a fifth that was rifled like a mould of a gun barrel; and a sixth that had an exterior steel baffler, a caricature of an arras – and a seventh and an eighth: a mini-Manhattan, most of which was still U/C, that my eye roved across desperate for repose, but found only the Burj itself, which seemed not to be the highest building in the world (with all the majesty that this would imply), but merely first among a rank of the equally banal.

I stopped in the middle of a dusty patch of waste ground to chat with Bhavuk from Bangalore. He waggled his bespectacled head with that Indian affirmative that seems such a denial that it's likely to end in auto-decapitation. He was a civil engineer and had been in Dubai for fifteen years – it was his home. He was still working, he conceded, although half of his workers had been laid off. He pointed out to me the tower he was erecting, which rose perhaps 600 feet to a four-sided pyramid, girded by a fretwork of stylised Ys. It would've been churlish to observe how trite it was, and besides, Bhavuk had no more responsibility for the building's form than an ant does for the shape of its heap – probably less.

I scuttled into the monstrous shadow of the development, a tinny mantra sounding in my ear: does form ever follow function, or has function kicked form to death? Loos viewed architectural ornamentation as 'criminal', but what can you say of an epoch in which the predominant style is not merely the theft and bowdlerisation of the ornamentation of the past, but the transmogrification of office buildings into gigantic knick-knacks. Even if these lipsticks and CD towers were finished and filled to the brim with people slaving over hot computer terminals, what would that say about them? For if the property asset bubble had gone on swelling, these myriads would only be skimming the froth off the aerated Starbucks of global trade; form ever follows function, and the function of these skyscrapers was surely only the replication of themselves: girders thrust into lift shafts in a grisly self-insemination of the built environment?

Except that Downtown Dubai was far from full to the brim – from a mile off I could sense its aching vacuity, the square miles of untrodden carpet tiling, the echoing atria and drained ornamental ponds. *At AED 2,500 per square foot, this is an opportunity not to be missed to buy in the most exclusive address in town: Downtown Dubai!* Dream on, Sheikh Mo, focus your visionary gaze on the far horizon. Can you see them out there, a Lost Tribe of suckers to replace the ones that have already fled? And then it came – the consummation, although not exactly the one I had so devoutly desired; this was to be no empowering humanisation of the world, nor nostalgic triumph of the eotechnic – I had yoked my psyche to Jim Ballard's visionary gaze, and so the Metro-Centre spake unto Downtown Dubai, a conversation that required no human intermediary. They whispered of their hollowness as they shifted in the wind, feeling the bronchitic pain of their ducts and vents; and they moaned of their ruination – windows burst, façades cracked, bony girders exposed – and they foresaw their death: a snaggle-toothed row of corpses silhouetted against a bloody sunset.

It was inevitable that I would be repelled as I tried to storm the bastion of Downtown Dubai, turned back by the monoxide-filled moat of the Sheikh Zayed Road, another six-lane highway, complete with elevated section and metro line U/C, which was walled off from the adjacent roads by continuous concrete crash barriers. I limped on along the sidewalk past the Crowne Plaza Hotel, and when I realised that the footbridge I'd been aiming for was also U/C, I diverted into Harman Electronics. By the entrance a 42-inch flat-screen television displayed an un-flickering, brushstroke-perfect *Afternoon Siesta* (1889) by Vincent van Gogh, the peasants curled into one another in the shadow of the hurting gold haystack. There was a stilted conversation with Achintya from Kerala and Amram from Manila about how to cross the road: I should get a cab – failing that two buses. If I insisted on walking there was a foot tunnel back by the Plaza. But I felt so weary, a weariness that yawned between the three of us there, in Harman Electronics, where business was – Achintya conceded – 'Very bad'.

I turned my back on the Emerald City of Downtown Dubai and marched determinedly away, down through Satwa, skirting the upscale residential district of Al Wasl, until I reached Jumeirah and the coast road. For the next four hours I only stopped by petrol stations to buy energy drinks then crouched, the sweat rapidly cooling on my hands, to check out the map displays, searching for the elusive Map 5. I passed the desiccated corpse of a cat, I passed racks of magazines, *OK Middle East* featured the nuptials of terminal cancer case and former Brit reality TV star Jade Goody. I passed the Jumeirah Beach Club where extended families of most hues cooked out at barbecue tables on cool swathes of green grass – and I cursed myself, yet again, for a fool and a masochist: I could've been with the girl-woman, who had told me she would be spending the weekend driving in the mountains of Oman.

DUBAI FLYOVER

I passed by a display of falcon statues, each one decorated by a local artist – *Shaping the Future* by Saidi Ali Nasser, who had covered the bird in sub-Paul Klee abstraction drew my particular opprobrium. I passed by Hummers – and I refined my hatred for the Cadillac Escalade, although perhaps it's merely petty to kick a 6-litre, V8 luxury sports utility vehicle when it's already down, its manufacturer burning up US government loans as readily as the car itself does petrol. I passed by an entire development of mock-traditional villas, each with its square wind tower and Moorish detailing, and gained an empty public beach from where I could look up and down the coast, but when I tried to head along it I was driven back inland by a private yacht club. I passed by the Miraj Art Centre and Saga World, I passed by a series of mosques that were U/C, their black hides yet to be concealed beneath white marble cladding, the signs of the British contractors – Balfour Beatty – standing proud. 'As I rode along I reflected that nowhere in the world was there such continuity as in the Arabian desert.' Thanks, Wilf. I heard the muezzin, and half-wished I could join them; someone once said to me: 'I pray on my knees, because it reminds me I'm not driving the car.'

I stopped to chat with some jolly Iranians who ran a shop selling inflatable goats – and when I went on again it was dusk; up ahead were fountains of lights in among the palms, more fruiterer's grass, and the steel-banded bluish-dune-shape of the Jumeirah Beach Hotel rose in the darkness to obscure the proud dhow-sail-shaped Burj Al Arab Hotel on its own purpose-built island. Inside these two eminences the rich were a-spending and the whores were a-whoring and the flunkeys were a-flunkeying, while back by the Burj Dubai, in the World Trade Centre, a rapt audience of 3,000 – including doting daddy, Sheikh Mo – were settling down to hear the Crown Prince, His Highness Sheikh Hamdan Bin Mohammed Bin Rashid Al Maktoum, '. . . recite', as the report in the *Gulf News* later put it, 'odes dripping with patriotism and love'. Sheikh Hamdan writes under the nom de plume Fazza'a, which means 'one who rushes to help people and save their lives'. I've since been unable to source an English translation of any of He Who Rushes to Help People and Save their Lives's verses – which, like those of his father, are composed in the Nabati Arabic vernacular – but judging from Sheikh Mo's own efforts: 'From anguish and woe of solitude, I shed / Tears of yearning, one after another', they may – I stress *may* – lose something in translation.

On Jumeirah Road the buses were picking up one shift of small brown tired men and dropping off another, slightly fresher one. The night was sodium and smog and engine revs, a fat man on a fat Harley Davidson pulled a wheelie – the sense of frenzy on the edge of a void was palpable. The Burj Al Arab came into view; up there on its crow's nest of a helipad Andre Agassi and Roger Federer had played an exhibition tennis match. The Al Arab styles itself as the only seven-star hotel in the world, by night it looks like a great white grub, crawling up into the heavens. I went on beside high walls behind which the palaces of the sheikhs loitered in shrubbery, while up ahead the final insult of the day stood above my destination: twin fake Chrysler Towers glittering in the night sky, beyond them the gleaming aluminium-clad hollowness of Dubai Media City, Dubai Marina and the Emirates Hills developments.

There was tarmac running into Knowledge City, but no sidewalk yet – I finished my day's walk on builders' sharp sand. I skipped under ropes strung between cones, and limped into the Holiday Express Inn. I was miserable, exhausted and defeated – Sheikh Mo had trounced me with his nightmarish vision. *Are you screwing me out?!* as we bellow in south London. He hovered in the lobby before me, his black gatefold beard clamped his saturnine mouth in its hairy creases – I wouldn't want to get on the wrong side of him: 'Oh, Sheikh Mo, do you know, a thousand five-dollar-a-day men have died / To build these 29.5 million square feet of office space?' would've been my contribution to the Festival – dripping with traitorous animosity, while scrupulously retaining the traditional metre of classical Arabic poetry.

I was alone in the dining room: Bijjar from Baluchistan brought bread and croutons for the lentil soup, while I read the *Gulf News*. The bread was oval segments of French sticks such as you might get anywhere in the world – the butter was in foil-covered plastic containers. The newspaper was full of anodyne small-town guff, interspersed with syndicated articles on the rise of Israeli nationalism – somewhat as if the *Brighton Evening Argus* took a surprisingly Arabist editorial line. I asked Bijjar for some local bread, and when it came – folds of liver-spotted discs – I had Thesiger-style rations, for when he crossed the Empty Quarter with the Rashid tribesmen, they took only bags of flour that they baked in the sand beneath the embers of a fire. According to Wilf, this unleavened bread was 'brick hard or soggy depending on how long it had been cooked, and always tasted as if it had been made from sawdust'.

You will die in a hotel room – I will die in a hotel room; we will all die in a hotel room, because at the moment of death – with Larry King on CNN, looking like Kermit the Frog, and with the angels playing the worst muzak ever – you, me – we – will all realise that our accommodation has always been temporary. I showered in the desalinated Arabian Sea, turned off the air conditioning and swooned in the

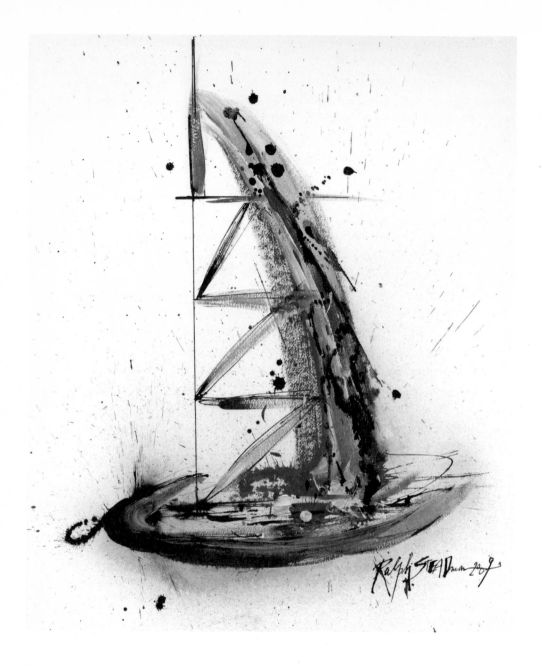

homogeneity. Dawn swam down to me through dynasties of dreams – couplings of eunuchs and multiple wives, real-estate agents hard-selling me office space in the seraglio – I went to the window and looked out across the residential suburb of Al Sufouh, to where on the horizon sunlight gilded the Burj Al Arab, and for a moment you could almost believe it was a minaret and this was a populous city with a human scale.

Until I stepped from the door of the Inn, and crunched my way across the sand and aggregate; until I looked back and saw the swathes of light and shadow draped from the hulk of Sheik Zayeed University building; until I felt the awful chilly nullity of the vertical desert rising behind me, and until I sidestepped the heavily masked helot on the miniature digger, I wasn't by any means certain that I'd actually have the nerve to press on, through that strange city of unbecoming, then into the sands beyond. I had a few folds of last night's flat bread, a banana, and two litres of water – my objective was twenty-two miles away, or so I estimated. It was 8 a.m. and the sun set at six in the evening. But if I'd hesitated on the brink, once I was walking the environment itself propelled me forward: there was no way to head south other than the hard shoulder of the D611, a six-lane expressway that swept up into overpasses, the entire weight of which pressed down on my pipsqueak body.

I pelted across the mouths of slip roads, scampering as herds of Escalades came thundering past, and passed over torture gardens where, soon enough, the myriad petunias would be boiled in their beds. The rampart of the Emirates Hills fell away behind me – inconceivably vast, so much bigger than I could have imagined. This seven-mile-long massif of steel, glass, aluminium and concrete was claimed to have an occupancy rate of 74 per cent (office), 70 per cent (residential) and 100 per cent (retail), although analysts conceded 'there are pockets where vacancy is far higher'. Pockets! Pah! I could *feel* the emptiness, feel it prickle the hairs on the nape of my neck. The intention had been to add another 70 million square feet of office space, a further 190,000 residential units and to roll out 30 million more square feet of shopping mall – but now . . . Well, now, projections across the board had been reduced by 50 per cent, and the very neatness of this, the exact halving, made the whole thing quite unbelievable: you don't *halve* a bubble, you don't neatly slice its inflexible skin. If you try and do this – pass the cut-throat razor across the eye, try it! – then there isn't a collapse, there's nothing; a few soapy specks, a splash of vitreous fluid – nothing.

I would not have given the Emirate Hills the honour of bearing my weight – even if there was a chance of them admitting me to their gated community, an exclusive preserve that numbers among its notable residents the family of Benazir Bhutto (deceased). The fleecers and those they've fleeced kept apart only by security guards and razor wire – wasn't it always thus? Nor would I have wished to stroll about the Dubai Pearl, were it existent, for the ambience of this – and so many of the other Dubai developments – is perfectly conveyed by the virtual tours on the developers' websites. *Step into the Pearl! Designed with people in mind.* Really, is that instead of extraterrestrials, or gnus? *100% pedestrian friendly, "walkable" and climate-controlled city.* It's the double quotes around "walkable" that do it to me, that and the *14,500 parking bays.* Trust me, as you live and breathe – you'd feel like a ghost in the Pearl, moving from mall to parking lot to lift; a point without extension, a free-floating Point Of View, so you might as well let your mouse do the actual walking through this, very Ballardian, inner space.

Besides, most of this is never going to be built, while much of what has been is only to a sixty-year specification – there was never any real aspiration to posterity in Sheikh Mo's vision, nor that of his anointed developers; in the argot, they had 'built to flip' – whack it up, flog it on, trouser the profit. In my more fervid moments I considered what Thesiger had said sixty years before: 'To arrange three stones as a fireplace on which to set a pot was the only architecture that many of [the Bedouin] required. They lived in black tents in the desert, or in bare rooms devoid of furnishings in the villages and towns. They had no taste nor inclination for refinements.' And I wondered if all this destruction-in-waiting was only the perpetuation by heftier means of this Bedu propensity to gorge then fast. The bubble will probably inflate once more – although whether it will ever again be so taut I doubt – but within a lifetime the oil to fuel this simulacrum of the temperate zone will be gone, the fountains will piddle to a finish, the air conditioners clatter to a halt, the skyscrapers, and the mock-mock-mock-Palladian villas, will begin to disintegrate, the artificial eminences they stand upon will start to crumble; the pseudo-pools, fake lagoons and ersatz rills will choke with sand – and so the western escarpment of Dubai City will subside into the Empty Quarter. In the 2000s it boasted the only seven-star hotel in the world – in the 2060s it will indeed be the eighth wonder of the world: its greatest and most futile ruin.

It was to experience this postmodernist ruination in a single day that I forced myself on along D611, already the convection was making a wavering mockery of road signs that pointed the way to 'The Greens', 'The Lanes' and 'The Springs'; already the half-built tower blocks and foundation pits bristling with thickets of steel, had the peculiar vibe of deconstruction. I stopped to chat with Dharma, a Nepalese civil engineer: 'Maybe half my workers have nothing to do now,' he said. Again: the 50 per cent. Did he, I wondered, really believe all these things would be built? 'Oh, certainly,' he replied unhesitatingly. 'They are all planned, you see.' But when I taxed him with my vision of a rusting United Arab Emirates, drained of its oily lifeblood, Dharma rambled into a riff: 'They are developing these alter-

DUBAI IN THE SKY ...

native technologies, you know – the solar power, the wind power . . . but I don't know . . . maybe they will not have enough of this in time.'

Around us the Pakistanis, the Baluchis and the Sudanese, their faces swathed in *keffiyeh*, unbolted the putlocks and clamps then loaded the poles on to the trucks. They jack-hammered the concrete to smithereens, then diggers scraped it up and dumped it into more trucks. The trucks wheeled out on to the highways, and as the convoy headed for the port at Jebel Ali the tarmac rolled up behind them.

This Dharma was at the junction of the D611 and the E44 Al Khail Road. There was, of course, no pedestrian crossing, but as I took my life in my hands to sprint across four lanes, recoup behind concrete crash barriers on the median strip, then dash across four more, I noticed that ahead of me the roadway – which on my map (published in 2008) was marked as fully achieved – was no more than a track for construction vehicles, that curled over the brow of a hill. I felt the land herself shift and shrug, as she asserted the primacy of her deeply sensual topography against the adolescent fumblings of Man. There were a couple more miles: an isolated mad erection, and a row of Palladian apartment blocks, the last one of which was painted a vile lemon-yellow, then an unashamed sign for the Sports City Labour Camp took me to the right. I began to count my paces: two, four, six . . . up to tens, then hundreds. Past a weary man with a heavy canteen who crouched, seeking refuge from the noonday sun, in the deep shadow of a dumper truck. Past the labour camp, where the air-conditioning units bolted to the Portakabins were almost as big as the accommodation itself and duty rosters flapped in the mephitic gusts from a Portaloo.

On a rise, beside a rubble heap, looking down over an open sewer littered with trash, I got out my compass and took a bearing on the crane to my rear, then projected it forward, south a kilometre or so, to where scrub bobbled a dune. In the mid-distance a man was submitting to a haircut – I could see the shed locks on his shoulders – while off to one side reposed the outsize bobbin of a discarded cable reel. I hitched up my pack, took a swig of water, shoved a plug of tobacco under my camel lip, and set off into the empty desert . . .

. . . Which wasn't empty at all; while I was obliged to maintain my southwards trek without deviating, there were no such strictures on the disorientated developers, who had bulldozed tracks, shoved up mounds, planted long lines of three-stranded, six-foot-high barbed wire fencing and generally laid waste to the wasteland. To plot a straight course across this scumbled terrain was bewildering; all the clean lines of the desert – the knife-edges of dunes and their exposed ribbing, the scribbled tussocks of salt bushes – had been blurred. I had to plough through white bull dust then dig my way under the fences. Thesiger wrote of the peace of the desert, the contemplation engendered by a pace slow enough to enable him – from the hump of his mount – to meditate on an isolated plant or rock for what seemed like hours. I too was fixated, but first on Donald Judd steel boxes, strewn across the *bled*, then a Twix wrapper half-obliterated by sand, and finally my bearing, which was now on a pylon in the distance that held open its steely arms to me, ready to give a 20,000-volt hug.

After an hour I reached the pylon and a road that should've been a major highway but which was only U/C, and thronged with dumper trucks. I stopped under a tree – the first shadow I'd come across – and improvised my own *keffiyeh* from my wicking T-shirt. I put on my long-sleeved shirt, and pulled my cloth cap down hard on my headdress – I was covered top to toe, but the sun was relentless, and my hands resembled a lobster's claws. A man came ambling up to the tree and muttered a few words of Urdu – clearly it was his shadow. I made as if to leave, but he gestured that I should remain, took a plastic bag that was dangling from a twig, and moved to the next tree along.

It was after 1 p.m., and if the incoherent map of the inchoate territory was even slightly reliable, I was already falling behind. Stuck under my tree, in Beckettian non-communication with my fellow shadow dweller, I considered, yet again, jacking it in – what was the *point*? But the thought of negotiating passage out of there – what could I do? Call in a targeted cab strike? – was almost worse, and so I went on. And on – it wasn't until mid-afternoon that I reached the last encampment of cranes and concrete-pourers. What was this? Possibly the beginnings of the Dubai World City, a fringe development of the new airport. I dug my way under yet another fence and found a pristine strip of newly built highway, across which padded a herd of feral camels; beyond this were more mounds of white bull dust which filled my shoes, then the beginnings of the Arabian Canal. Abdullah – I assume this was his name, it was blazoned on the side of his tanker – was pumping something into a pipeline in the twenty-foot-deep trough. He was unmistakably an Emirati, from his headdress to his worry beads.

I approached the tanker. 'Salaam Al-Alaikum,' I placed my hand on my heart as I said this; predictably a less than satisfactory exchange ensued, given that this was my only Arabic. Still, Abdullah spoke the lingua franca of directions perfectly well: I wanted to get to Bab Al Shams? That was easy enough – I should simply head back up the new strip of highway, head east on the D57 and then it was a right off there. How far? Not far, maybe thirty minutes' drive . . . But – and here I mimed

49

with my fingers – I was *walking*, so would this be the right direction? Absolutely! Abdullah was quite certain, and what was more betrayed no surprise that I should be travelling in such a fashion, so I crossed the Arabian Canal (U/C), climbed another manmade dune, and found myself at long last in the desert proper.

The final human detritus I saw before being swallowed up by the sands was a gashed sack of curiously bright red nuggets; somehow, I immediately connected these in my mind with the feral camels: it's a poison, I thought. They're poisoning the camels so they don't fuck with the airport construction – that's why that camel shit there looks so red . . . and that's why there's the corpse of a camel over there, its ribs protruding from the tatters of its red skin . . . and that's why the very sands are vermilion – they're contaminated too! It wasn't until a week or so later, when I looked at the photographs I'd taken of the sands, that I realised that the ruddy tinge was in my own eye – the beginnings of a mild heatstroke that left me with glowing motes orbiting my eyeballs and nausea that came and went for days.

However, at the time I took the vermilion sands in my stride, as a visible – and even tangible – proof of the success of my mission: behind me Dubai City was crumbling into the red dust, and now, as the sun began to sink to the horizon, I was free to continue south into a primordial world. A sand fox, up early, skittered away into a wadi, then, as I reached the top of the next acclivity, six ibex came barrelling along the side of the one beyond. So fast! As fast as *cars*, their front legs punching up high at the air as they bullied their way forward. At last I was transported into Thesiger's contemplative space, where a squiggle of dead convolvulus could enthral me for the long minutes it took me to reach it. I bent down to observe the liquid motion of blown sand on the face of a dune; I savoured the contrast between the hard-packed sand on the windward faces and the powder on the sheltered side. I went on across a rollicking sea of peaks and troughs, soon falling into an easy rhythm: checking my compass bearing on a distant tumulus at the top of each rise, then adjusting my focus to bush after bush, as it was lost from sight.

I had what my mother would've termed 'a deep Semitic intuition' about this tumulus, which was the only darker feature I could make out in the tan expanse: it lay on my southerly bearing and looked to be about six or seven miles off. I even fancied there were date palms on top of it – surely this was my 2,300 dhiram-a-night oasis, Bab Al Shams? But actually, I didn't really mind if it wasn't; in fact, I concluded it had been craven of me to have booked a hotel at all – a night out in the desert would do me good. True, the last time I'd slept out alone in the desert, it had been the Tanami in Northern Australia, and all night I'd been plagued by goannas charging through my campsite, but that was a quarter of a century ago – I was a less timorous beastie now.

On the other hand, I had been walking for almost ten hours – I was footsore, filthy and dehydrated, with only a few mouthfuls of water left in my bottle. Stopping for a smoke under a dead tree I gave in to Sheikh Mo's vision and switched on my phone to see if there was a signal. It peeped horribly in the fastness – I had missed a local call. I called whoever it was back, and Crystal materialised out of the ether. Crystal was – she informed me in unmistakable Lancashire tones – the duty manager of the Bab Al Shams Hotel, and she thought she ought to give me a call to warn me that since it was the Prophet's birthday no alcohol would be served in any of the three restaurants that evening; nor would there be the usual traditional Arabian entertainment. I replied that this wasn't a problem for me on either count, but there was one thing she could help me with: was Bab Al Shams surrounded by trees? Yes, yes, she said, it was – but why did I want to know?

I explained about the walk and was met with the usual silent incredulity that, over the years, I've grown accustomed to. It no longer excited me, no longer made

LOCAL CAMEL

me feel privileged or subversive – it was just a drag, talking to people who didn't really know where they were. Crystal was professionally amiable, and suitably impressed once I'd convinced her that I was out in the desert, with night fast falling, having trekked all the way from Dubai City. 'I might need to call again,' I said. 'If the trees I'm aiming towards aren't yours.'

Of course, the cell phone had ruined it all: the ibex, the dunes – the desert. I was yanked back from the vermilion sands into a world of bloody-mindedness: the economic prerogatives of supply and demand, hierarchy and subjection. I tried to savour the miles that were left to me – but I was alone no more, there were 4WD tracks on the formerly pristine sand, and after an hour's more walking, I came up to the hundred-foot-high tumulus – it wasn't the hotel, only a lookout tower in a plantation of date palms, around which swirled a dirt road. Doubtless this was some piece of tourist infrastructure – a Desert Experience that had already been constructed. Beyond, at the bottom of a wide shallow valley, there was a straggle of buildings covering several miles. Floodlights were already illuminating what looked like a racetrack.

I could have aimed for any part of this development, and doubtless eventually discovered the hotel – but the Nokia had robbed me of my strength and it would soon be completely dark. I called Crystal back and explained what I could see from the hill. 'I'm a little confused,' she admitted, 'because the country around the hotel is basically flat.'

'Obviously it seems flat if you only ever *drive* across it – ' I began to admonish her, but then gave up – why *bother*? And besides, I could see some fake Arabian towers in among a host of palms that *had* to be a desert resort, so I hung up on Crystal and continued, maintaining – with some satisfaction – the southern bearing I had first started walking along at eleven that morning. A full moon rose in the direction of Mecca. I dug my way under a fence, reached a fake caravanserai that I deduced – quite rightly – must be an arena where the hotel staged pseudo-Bedouin horse extravaganzas, then, following a virulent pink-surfaced road lined with date palms, passed a steel barn with a back-lit electric sign in front of it: 'QUARANTINE STABLES 3, AUSTRALIA, NEW ZEALAND', and found myself in a perfectly ordinary car park.

Two words on luxury: it sucks. It can never achieve the warm yumminess of mummy's womb; no mattress will ever provide as much repose as the cushion of her amniotic fluid; no cuisine will ever taste as sweet – nor be served so expeditiously – as the blood pumped through your umbilicus. Yet all luxury aspires to the condition of the womb: muffling sounds, softening surfaces and providing service that is at once instant, personalised, and yet utterly faceless. Besides, why pay for infantilisation when it costs nothing to pule? Why pay to be unable to do anything for yourself when poverty can provide exactly the same experience of deprivation? The man who put out his hand beseechingly in the shadow of the Burj Dubai, showing his rotten yellow teeth as he implored for a few coins – was he not the beneficiary of as much luxury as the wealthy guests at Bab Al Shams? Like the very rich, nothing much interests the very poor save for where their next meal is coming from.

In the warm, woody lobby at Bab Al Shams, under the visionary eyes of Sheikh Mo (in oils), the receptionist swiped my credit card, Crystal chatted to me, and a servitor brought me first a warm damp towel, and latterly an ice-cold Coca-Cola. My plastic water bottle instantly evaporated. Sheikh Mo had, Crystal told me, ordained that all new construction projects in the Emirate should be finished by 2015. I observed that by then the appellation 'desert resort' would hardly be applicable to Bab Al Shams, what with the cranes swarming towards it over the dunes, and she conceded that the peripheral development of Al Maktoum International Airport would, indeed, be visible from where we were sitting. What then, I thought, of Sheikh Mo's vision? After all, this was the man who gained – or so he assured us – his great sense of perseverance from the very desert itself, yet within his poxy Emirate – the border lay only a few miles further south – if he persevered there would be no desert left.

Crystal, who was indeed from Preston, Lancashire, seemed philosophic about it all: twelve of her own friends had quit Dubai in the last three months – but she enjoyed her forty-minute commute out to the hotel from the city, and business was . . . well, holding up. True, it was Sunday night – and the Prophet's birthday to boot – but as Crystal led me to my room through a labyrinth of passages the hotel had the sepulchral ambience of a rock-cut tomb. And the colour scheme: Bab Al Shams was a muted symphony of tan, terracotta umber, burnt sienna and other earthy tones. In my womby-tomby room brass whatnots glowed in niches, and the bedside lamp was a dangling brass-and-glass lantern that barely shed enough light to decipher the numerals on the TV remote – let alone read a stock report.

There were a few Emirati men standing out on the terrace smoking, and in the gloom their white robes and headdresses made them look like the Hattifatteners in Tove Jansson's 'Moomintroll' kids' books – tall, pale creatures, attracted to lightning. I ate dinner in the empty Al Forsan ('the Horseman') Restaurant, feeling like Dave, the astronaut in Kubrick's *2001*, who, having touched down on Ganymede, finds himself standing in the corner of a luxury hotel suite, watching his aged self dining in a dressing gown, under the watchful eye of a featureless obelisk. Actually, in fairness to Al Forsan, I often feel like Dave in 2001 – my breathing whooshing in my ears as if I were scuba diving on land, my visual field glassy and binocular, the cutlery clattering loudly, my sense of self flickering between depersonalisation and psychosis. The featureless obelisk approaches soundlessly: 'Is everything all right, sir?' receives assurance and retreats.

And that's luxury too: the pressing need for mutual reassurance between server and served. Not that the waiters in Al Forsan were featureless obelisks, and neither is this a sample dialogue:

'Is everything all right, sir? Is this Premier Cru Beurval butter in its individual foil-lidded tub to your taste?'

'*Mais, oui! Assurement.*'

'Are you ready to order now, sir?'

'I'd like the mixed kebab – but is there any vegetable with that?'

'There's rice, won't that satisfy you, you fat fuck? After all, you'll be packing in more meat than my family – wife and three small children who, incidentally, I've only seen three times in the last six years – have in a month.'

But it might as well have been. The fireflies swarmed in my face mask, the meat fell down my oesophagus and rotted in the Empty Quarter of my belly. The muzak was Arabian-electro, it sounded like someone doing something unspeakable to a camel with a cattle prod. I stared warily about me at the oil paintings of ramping Arabian stallions: 'Is everything all right, sir?' And patted the hump of the wooden camel that was couched in the niche by my table: 'Is everything all right, sir?' And called for the bill: 'Was everything all right, sir?'

It took me three attempts to get back to my room. Crystal had warned me that the layout of the hotel could be 'confusing' – but I found it utterly bewildering, with its maze of shrubbery-choked courtyards, flowery bowers and ornamental ponds, connected by earthenware tunnels. I kept finding myself back in the lobby, and eventually – perhaps this was only a fitting 'luxury' – I had to be led to bed.

In the night Dion A. Liveras came sailing into the room in his giga-yacht and moored alongside my barque of sleep. According to the *Gulf News*, Dion and his yacht *Alysia* would be one of the star attractions at the forthcoming Abu Dhabi Yacht Show. 'The five decks are connected by a guest lift,' breathlessly incanted associate editor Samir Salama. 'And a separate lift whisks staff from one level to another so as to be practically invisible. The yacht has four Jacuzzis, including one on deck and another in the spa with its fibre-optic star ceiling and glass panels that subtly change colour and broadcast song emanating from an early morning avian orchestra.'

Yes, Salama had nothing but praise for the British Cypriot businessman; or, as he more elegantly styled Liveras, the 'confectioner-turned-luxury yacht charter business owner' who had taken the tiller after his father was killed during the Mumbai terrorist attacks. You might have thought that this horror would have imposed upon Liveras a re-evaluation of at least one or two of his values – but there was no room on board the *Alysia* for such scruples. 'His family's business elegantly defies the global recession,' panted Salama, who also reported the chartered confectioner's muscular assertion that: 'There are a lot of people in the world who have fortunes and are willing to spend big bucks.'

Morning revealed Bab Al Shams to be an island of artificial lawns surrounded by security fencing, against which the ceaseless waves of the soon-to-be-superannuated desert lapped. Back at Al Forsan the breakfast was of Arabian Nights proportions: *majjis* rooms full of suppliant dates, apricots and melon; an entire swooning harem of cereals, croissants and muffins. Since the resort had been temperately terra-formed, it seemed only appropriate to have a pork-free version of an English breakfast, complete with chicken sausages, veal bacon and camel's milk. Apart from the camel's milk it was all unspeakably vile. 'Is everything all right, sir?'

I sat in the torpor of my heat stroke cutting up the veal bacon – which had the consistency of car tyres – with my lobster claws. If I had wanted to walk back to The World I would've had to have left at 3 a.m., for my trip was scheduled for three that afternoon. There was nothing for it but to laze away the morning, then call in a targeted cab-strike.

# Two Fantasias on a Visionary Theme by Sheikh Mohammed bin Rashid Al Maktoum

## 1. The World

It would've been unreasonable to expect to be able to just steam in, and, having walked to The World, then fulfil my ambition of walking the length of the island of Britain – one of the 300 that make up this bizarre artificial archipelago. To begin with I hadn't walked all the way from Jim Ballard's house in Shepperton (barring the plane flight from Heathrow to Dubai International), but instead the arid wastes of Tiger Woods* had sapped my zeal, while the free-floating anniversary of the Divine Prophet had queered my timing. I quite liked the irony of a Jewish Anglican such as myself being barred access to a simulacrum of my homeland by a Muslim festival – it placed not just The World, but the world, in the right kind of perspective. Yet this was not the ultimate hurdle, which was merely the absence of a landing stage.

The PR from Nakheel, Sheikh Mo's property-developing subsidiary, was only too willing to assist me, but when we reached The World we found that the jetty had been towed across to Germany. Back in 2006, Richard Branson, the condom-'n'-cola magnate, had planted the Union flag on Britain – part of a publicity stunt to 'celebrate' the beginning of direct Virgin Airways services between London and Dubai. More recently, Piers Morgan, the egregious former *Daily Mirror* editor who had been dumb enough to buy faked photographs of squaddies torturing Iraqi captives (when there were so many real ones going the rounds), had also set foot on Britain for a TV travelogue he was filming.

Possibly I lacked the clout to have the landing stage shifted, still, I didn't want to make too much of a fuss, because frankly I thought it quite a coup to have got out to The World at all. True, I'd made no attempt to disguise my identity to the PR

---

* Four million gallons of water will be required weekly to irrigate this sand trap – if it's ever completed; each gallon's desalination generates as much in emissions as the equivalent volume of petrol. No wonder inhabitants of Dubai have a carbon footprint twice that of Americans.

– nor what I was intending to write about, so I could only imagine that either she'd not done her research at all thoroughly, or she and her masters felt that any negative coverage accruing from allowing me access would be less than that which might result from barring me.

Personally, were I in Nakheel's position I wouldn't have allowed me anywhere near this deranged exercise in miniaturism – a satirist's gift if ever there was one. I'd have launched tiny dreadnoughts to shell me out of the water, or mini-subs to torpedo me.

Still, I couldn't help but feel a little sorry for the unwitting – and frankly ovine – PR, who met me in the lobby of the Nakheel sales office (corporate slogan: 'Our vision inspires humanity'), where I sat a trifle uneasily beneath another portrait of the far-sighted ruler. After we'd exchanged greet-

A SATIRIST'S GIFT — WHAT??

ings, she led me into a large room full of architectural models. 'Ooh!' I exclaimed. 'I *love* models – sometimes I think they're better than the real thing.' 'Sometimes' is the operative word here: I don't prefer models of my wife and children to the family themselves, and nor do I yearn for a scale model of the Pantheon or the Parthenon – but when it comes to architecture as inane as that commissioned by Nakheel, shrinking it then sealing it in Perspex does, on the whole, seem to be the best option.

Of course, The World itself is a model, which raises the curious philosophic question of what a model of a model adds to the increased intelligibility of its subject that a simple model provides. Lévi-Strauss thought the miniature to be the archetypal form of the artwork, observing that even Michelangelo's frescos for the Sistine Chapel were miniatures, given that their subject matter was the Creation itself. The literalism and pictorial crudity of the Palm developments – which Nakheel have dubbed a 'trilogy', although 'copse' might be a better descrip-tor – also suggest, to me, a religious undertone – or rather, uneasily ambivalent Islamic recusance, embodying as they do two simultaneous and contrary urges: on the one hand to demonstrate that the world is without form until a Koranic instruction manual has been employed, and on the other to tickle the beards of the devout with what are – in essence – gross pictographs.

Indeed, once you begin observing the Arabian peninsula from the satellite perspective favoured by Sheikh Mo's vision, it's hard not to be gripped by the geopolitical dimension to all this: there are the United Arab Emirates and Oman – the instep and sole respectively – of a foot that's kicking the soft underbelly of Iran, Afghanistan and Pakistan. Or, possibly a more phallic protuberance (together with its priapic skyscrapers and lubrication of Western fast food fat, alcohol and sun cream), being thrust into the parted arse cheeks of the rest of the *umma* – an act of tectonic sodomy that might have been purposely calculated to inflame the honour of the Islamists. Not that there's anything in the least *gay* about the Emiratis themselves, unless they've changed in the last couple of generations. Thesiger conceded that homosexuality was 'common among most Arabs, especially in the towns'. However: 'it is very rare among the Bedu . . . They sometimes joked about goats, but never about boys'.

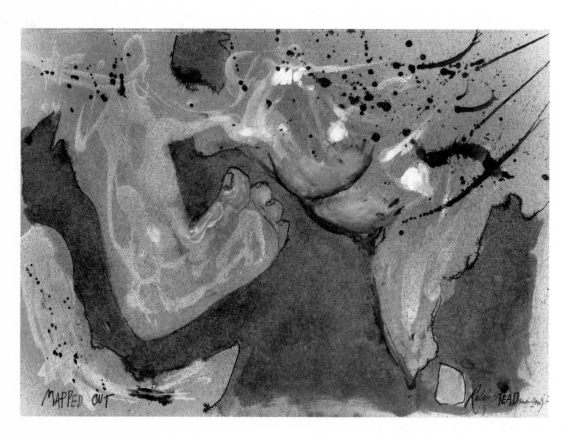

MAPPED OUT

I thought back to the jolly Iranians and their inflatable ones, but joking about goats aside, there was little to laugh at as the PR and I climbed aboard the launch – which was crewed by a pair of the most dapper Dravidians I've ever seen – and the engines were started. The acceleration was rapid, and soon enough we were banging across the wave crests with our wake curling behind us, like a classic Arabian calligraphic descender. The fake Chrysler Towers of Knowledge City shrank as we tended away from the long bulk of the Palm and swept by Logo Island, an autonomous luxury development that – to my oikish eyes – looked a little like a cement factory. Logo Island! A name to conjure with. There are in fact a pair of Logo Islands, one either side of the Palm's trunk, and to Sheikh Mo SatVis they clearly resemble stylised – hugely stylised – Nakheel logos; a logo which is effected by the still further stylisation of the Arabic characters for 'Nakheel'. Neat, eh?

The dapper crew, the spotless launch, the sparkling sea, the girl more or less straight from a public relations degree course at a provincial British university; I could be forgiven, surely, for imagining I was on my way to the secret island of Dr Mo – or possibly Dr Mo(reau) – where I would be subjected to appalling vivisection: my legs amputated and my brain replaced with that of a property developer. From the sea the Palm Jumeirah's barrier wall looked precisely like what it was: seven million tons of rock. It beggared belief that the planners of this five-by-five-kilometre spit hadn't realised that if you almost completely enclosed such a large patch of sea water it would rapidly become stagnant – but they hadn't. However, they'd got round this problem by punching another channel in the barrier, and now – or so their tame marine biologists claimed – the interstices of the Palm's seventeen fronds were notable for the rich biota: sea grass, reef fish, oysters – the whole tropical collation. Not that residents of the Palm would be expecting anything quite so farouche; scuba diving is to take place around the submerged hulks of two F-100 Super Sabre jets (as flown by the USAF in Vietnam), and it was also written that a one-kilo gold bar had been sunk on the seabed of this pleasure pool.

Possibly Hamid Karzai – a Palm property-owner – or his allegedly smack-dealing brother, would enjoy stripping off, plunging into the warm waters and searching for the loot. It would make a nice change from coping with the hugger-mugger of frondlife – let alone Kabul. Karzai's gaff is bang opposite that of Kieron Dyer, the West Ham footballer – just two of the 8,000 residences that have been shoe-horned onto the Palm, instead of the 4,500 originally planned for. Those who had pre-bought their houses were unceremoniously informed of the new zoning two years before the Palm's completion – of course, at that time, with the bubble rapidly inflating, few of them complained (not that they had any recourse);

however, now Palmatians were watching their equity gold dust blowing away in the wind, the mutterings of discontent were growing louder.

Personally, I think if you buy a house on a manmade twenty-five-kilometre-square palm-shaped peninsula you've got the wrath of God coming to you, and to then – as one resident is quoted as saying – complain that: 'It was absolutely nothing like as it was depicted in the brochure', invites a very humanitarian derision. Hell, even Nakheel's own consultant environmentalist was moved to remark – while defending the Trilogy development overall – that, 'There is a philosophical question as to whether habitat creation through rocky reefs, sea grass meadows and extensive inter-tidal beaches (70km on Palm Jumeirah) is sufficient mitigation for our island building activities.' Indeed, and the philosophical answer to that question was provided summarily by the tower cranes that stood idle where work on the $2.96 billion (estimated cost) Trump International Tower had ceased. 'Ordinary is for other people' read the billboard in front of these cranes – which may well be the very gibbets upon which civilisation will be hung. Yes, ordinary is

ATLANTIS

for other people, and we'll take it quite happily rather than repair to the Atlantis, a seven-star luxury hotel that has all the architectural finesse of a fat rich fuck sitting on your face. Besides – who in their right mind would name a hotel after a mythical land that was catastrophically inundated, let alone check into one? So, the Atlantis, where every guest room has either a sea view, or one of a shark tank, stands empty and mouldering.

Out in the open sea, the man at the wheel cranked up the engines and the launch shifted from banging over the wave crests to whacking through them. The entire coastline of Dubai was revealed to me wreathed in its brownish smogosphere: from the downtown blocks around the creek, to the pinnacles of Downtown Dubai and the bodkin of its Burj, to the maggoty Burj Al Arab and then along to the sky-infestation of the Dubai Marina development. That, I thought, is the world in all its teeming, besmirched obsolescence, while up ahead is The World: deserted, and pristine, a bas-relief planet. Its sandy magma had been scoured from the seabed by Dutch creator-contractors Van Oord, then – using a technique known rather poetically as 'rainbowing', a reference to the arcs of spectrographic sludge – the nine-by-eight-kilometre lagoon had been gathered together in one place, and let the dry land appear: and it was so. And the Developer called the dry land The World, and He filled it with islets ranging from five to twenty acres, and each shaped like a much-loved portion of the old world – and the Developer believed they would be highly covetable.

Property prices on the Palm were down – you guessed it – 50 per cent in the last quarter, while out here The World was doing just fine: 70 per cent of the islets were sold, and the remaining 30 per cent were – or so Nakheel would have us believe – still hotly desired. During 2009, as in previous years, exclusive 'invitations to own The World' would be sent out to the lucky few. At least, that's how it was meant to work, although the allocation of Great Britain Island (as its current owner prefers to style it) seems to have been more problematic. Bought initially by a consortium from Galway, in the west of Ireland, who had already been 'invited to own' the Ireland island, Great Britain mysteriously floated – like Laputa – back into Nakheel's hands, and then was sold again, this time to Safi Qurashi, a British Asian property developer now based in Dubai.

Inside the barrier reef of The World the boatman cut the engines, we snaked between the sandy models of South America and Africa, then coasted into the lagoon of the North Atlantic, before – after about three minutes – rounding the Iberian Peninsula and puttering up the 'French' coast. The continents were all featureless sandbars – although I saw a Portaloo in the approximate region of Nigeria.

Developers had to get soil analyses done and apply for planning permission before they could begin turning the phantasmal real estate into rental income, but then – who knows? Everyone – including you: for while some are intent on solo luxury villas, others cleave to the sameness of 'mixed development'. The Irish consortium had intended the Britain island to be styled 'Greater Britain' and to slap down a luxury hotel together with 219 residential units, while their vision for the reunited British Isles saw the units on Ireland island – 'Ireland in the sun' – fetching from 850,000 to 3 million euros.

John O'Dolan joked at the time of his consortium's purchase, 'I have been asked if I plan on joining the two islands together.' He also couldn't forbear from a little Celtic crowing: 'We were honoured that Nakheel came to an Irish person to buy the island of England. There was lots of talk about Richard Branson and Rod Stewart wanting to buy it and there are some very annoyed people in England who thought they had it but didn't get it.' On 29 February 2009, John O'Dolan's body was found in a shed in the grounds of his property near Galway – the fifty-one-year-old father of three, apparently deeply troubled by the financial downturn, had taken his own life.

At his funeral Mass, Father Peter Finnerty – a friend since boyhood – alluded to the widespread suspicion in Ireland that the banks had acted savagely towards overexposed businesses. 'In all my years of knowing John, he never once reneged on a deal or let a debt go unpaid. I would like to ask the question . . . was John in any way singled out? Was he treated in any way unfairly that has brought us to this situation? I think it is a fair question to ask.'

I didn't know about O'Dolan's suicide when, nine days later, I leapt off the launch and on to the white coral sands of 'Germany'. Obviously I was disappointed not to be setting foot on 'Britain'; I had had it in mind to advance swiftly – *veni, vidi, vici*-style – walking from one end of the model landmass to the other, and so prefigure a walk the length of the real Britain that I was planning to take a couple of years hence. In the hopeful recesses of my mind – pinkish tissue bowers, sparking with neural luminescence – I imagined puttering the handful of paces from the south coast, across a Garden of England the size of a suburban garden; then discovering, laid out before me, a reconstruction of a Ballardian London: a herringbone pattern of pitched red roofs, the water feature of the Thames, beside it the rockery of the Chelsea Harbour gated development that Jim had hymned in *Millennium People*. Further along, the London Eye Ferris wheel would freewheel like a bike wheel, while further out buzzed a shrunken Heathrow, complete with cucumber-frame terminals and remote-control jets taxiing its tarmac paths.

OMAN ON SEA AND SKY

I advance carefully through the outskirts of 'London', stepping from municipal park to municipal park, until I see between my feet the familiar shape of Jim's own house, and there I was, on the far side of the miniature M3 motorway, an aphid struggling to extricate itself from a bramble patch, while in the near distance swelled the embankments of the reservoirs, and beyond these Vaughan cruised the arterial roads in search of another climactic collision, one that would mean . . . 'the intimate space and time of a single human being had been fossilized for ever in this web of chromium knives and frosted glass'.[*]

I had to make do with Germany – no South Seas atoll lorded over by new primitives, just the sandbar, the PR, and a tool chest left behind by a work party. We strolled about a bit, the PR bare-footed and with an armful of brochures – a Miranda in search of her satellite Aerial. I had no idea whether 'Germany' was owned by anyone, or remained *lebensraum*, ready for the taking. When I returned to the – putatively – real London I called Safi Qurashi and asked him why he'd bought Great Britain Island. 'Um, er, it kind of fitted in with the business strategy we have here in Dubai . . . that was one of the reasons. Also, patriotic reasons – having been born and brought up in south London . . . and the fact that I think The World development is quite unique and amazing.'

So, this son of Balham had bought 'Britain' for patriotic reasons – I laboured to cope with the elasticity of allegiance that could account for such sentiments. It certainly made a mockery of the campaign mounted by those who believed that British Muslims should be required to take some kind of loyalty test. Naturally, I wanted Qurashi to say he would be bucking the trend and creating a Ballardian myth of the near future, an exteriorisation of inner space, but instead he told me, 'We've got some concepts that we're working on . . . the idea is to create a mixed-use island which allows people to live, visit, enjoy the scenery around it, so, a small hotel, some apartments and villas, some commercial space . . . so it becomes the sort of place where if you're here on a holiday you can visit the island, if you want to you can live on it.' And I suppose this was a nice idea: a porous Great Britain Island, welcoming to immigrants and asylum seekers, rather than deporting them, or banging them up in high-security detention centres.

I asked Safi about the recession, and whether he was worried, and his answer made me picture him all the more as a curiously tweedy, conservative and emphatically under-exposed developer: 'It would be wrong to say that no one's worried about the downturn – but worried in terms of have we bought the right thing?

---

64    [*]  J. G. Ballard, *Crash* (1973).

No, not at all. We knew it was going to be a long-term, five- to seven-year development, so the fact that we're going to have to slow down a bit for a year, eighteen months – I think it's not a bad thing, the ability to slow down gives us more time to think, to breathe, to look at things from a different perspective, and hopefully we can come out of that with something a lot better, rather than running around as a lot of us were in the past three or four years, when you don't have the time to look to the future.'

This didn't really tally with the long article in that week's *Building News* that began by echoing my darkest visions: 'Dubai is looking more and more like a place with a great future behind it . . .' and went on to describe how the city-state had debts of $80 billion due to be paid in 2009, and this in an economy where, in recent years, 60 per cent of turnover had been from real estate – now developers were owing and contractors were owed. A lot. Safi, however, remained John Bullish: 'Is it any different to any other part of the world?' he said. 'I think you need to scratch a bit more underneath the surface here; Dubai fundamentals are very sound although construction has been a big part of increased income. Besides, you can manipulate the stats and look at them in a certain way.'

I didn't feel I could effectively counter such a gung-ho attitude with anything I had in my armoury; that's always been capitalism's great strength – its optimism: buy now! enjoy later! What on earth did I and my ilk have to offer save: realise now! we're fucked! Besides, Safi was a man who, despite wondering about the impact of global warming on his patriotic vision, had nonetheless been reassured that rising sea levels would have 'virtually no effect' on his low-lying, Dutch-created, pseudo-Britain. Canute-like, he was prepared to repel the waves with a great slick of oil revenue, the result of price inflation from an estimated $25 a barrel increasing threefold.

Stranger still, as our phone conversation mutated into a fulsome email correspondence I began to find myself oddly beguiled by Safi; here was a Britishness even I might be able to subscribe to: 'When you're reaching it from a sea level,' he wrote, 'it's so difficult to tell one island from another, so the idea has always been that as you approach the island there is a very British feel to it, when you're landing on it you feel that yes, you are in Great Britain . . . That doesn't mean that we would suddenly start replicating some iconic buildings – that's not what we want to do, but we'll certainly give it a look and a feel.'

A look and a feel – isn't that all you really want from a nation state? You can do without all the troublesome pretensions of tradition and nationalism enshrined in iconic buildings – let alone a political system. Dr Mo himself was on to the right approach with his version of Greenland, which, far from being a small-scale recreation of melting ice cap, snowmobile-borne Inuit and US military bases, had instead the look and feel of somewhere Leif Ericsson would've been delighted to make landfall: great stands of tropical plants and an opulent – but by no means vulgar – villa. The boatmen, who liked to get around The World at speed, took us for a swift Atlantic crossing, then a circumnavigation of its chilly affluence.

Then it was time to leave. The steersman cranked up the engines, and within minutes The World was lost from view beneath our foaming wake, while the world – which, throughout our stay, had hovered uneasily on the horizon – now expanded before us. Back there were the unpaid contractors and the malnourished *Gastarbeiter*, back there former Chechen warlords were being gunned down in underground car parks, back there the great spike of the Burj Dubai awaited to impale me.

I knew which version I preferred.

## 2. High Rise

I wanted to take a bus from the Nakheel sales offices by the Palm Jumeirah to the Mall of the Emirates, some five miles away – for me the walking was over, the cab ride in from the desert had torn through the enormously distended calf muscle that stretched all the way from Shepperton; from now on I would be taking Dubai on its own mechanised terms. You have to visit a shopping mall while you're in Dubai – if you don't (and don't spend at least 300 dhirams while you're there), Sheikh Mo's secret police, the Amn al-Dawla, will detain you and you may even be tortured. All right, I made this last bit up, the police only arrest people for crimes that are clearly on the statute book – adultery, dope, buggery – and they only flog someone or put them to death once in a blue moon. There are subtler forms of coercion at work in Dubai: a velvety rut for the natives, who get free everything until they express an independent opinion; and a dusty one for the helots, who no one will listen to anyway.

Besides, why bother to exact such cruel retribution when the traffic will do it for you? An American expatriate I spoke to told me that pedestrians are killed 'every week' scampering across the multi-lane highways, and is it fanciful to imagine that it is these people – whether through immiseration or ideology – who are the potential insurgents? After all, what can they be attempting to escape from save the deadening conformity of the mall, where the multiracial throng shuffles seven times around the glassy cabinet, pointing ritually at the desired object, while abandoned to the ecstasy of acquisition?

I wanted to get the bus, but the PR had no idea where I could. 'To be honest,' she vouchsafed, 'Europeans don't take them.' So she asked a brown colleague and he directed me towards the fake Chrysler Buildings of Knowledge City. I had to walk a mile up to the pedestrian crossing over the Al Sufouh Road, and when I reached the stop I found there wasn't a service directly there. Anyway, the men squatting in the shadow of the air-conditioned shelter didn't want me to take a bus – they seemed outraged by the idea of my broaching the transport colour bar, and bundled me unceremoniously into a cab driven by Zony from Swat in Pakistan.

Zony had seen his three children twice in the last six years: 'What can we do?' he said. 'We are poor people.' I asked him about the Swat regional government's recent concession to the local Taliban, allowing them to impose sharia law. 'I want religious system,' he said, 'but not for all people. It is like this, you are human – I am human . . .' I began, I confess, to tune out when I heard these words: on the face of it a decent proposition, a lowest common genetic denominator of morality

– but I didn't feel particularly human that afternoon, I'd just made landfall from another planet, and I had the starbursts of interstellar travel still popping in my eyes to prove it.

At the Mall of the Emirates a life-size stuffed giraffe was for sale and there were women wearing abayas chucking snowballs at each other at the bottom of the ski slope. I stood and watched them while an Emirati in white robes pressed himself against the back of an East European blonde in Lycra, his pretext: steadying her hand while she took a photograph of the black sacks shooting out white balls. This ski slope – complete with ski lifts, artificial evergreens and Swiss-chalet-style woodwork – is the crystalline essence of all thinking concerning Dubai's exponential growth. For critics it is the *dernier cri* in wastefulness, as well as an anti-natural folly to rival anything a Des Esseintes might contrive; while for the boosters this is the material form of the Emirate's chutzpah: a carney shtick that wouldn't be out of place on Coney Island.

For my part, the ski slope of the Mall of the Emirates had no more impact than my own fridge – it was just another big icebox full of human leftovers ('I'm ham – you're ham'). If it had any significance it was that here was a large artificial environment inside another still vaster artificial environment – the mall itself. By no stretch of the imagination were Esprit, Bulgari and Borders to be found naturally occurring on the Trucial Coast – their climate control required quite as much power and desalinated water to function as the 300 feet of powder the Puffa jackets slid down. Like The World, the ski slope was a model of a model – a reduction that allowed the disinterested observer to see the ideal of human progress writ painfully small. But then I'm by no means the ideal customer for these, ahem, facilities – I was underwhelmed by the Brent Cross Shopping Centre, which, when it opened – in 1976 – was then the biggest mall in Britain with a piffling 74,620 square metres of retail space and concourses. Indeed, I struggle to cross these wastes of tiling, and whenever I enter a mall I worry that I may either suffer a heart attack and collapse in a water feature, or, having bought a small ornamental glass bowl, repair to the toilets – last cleaned thirty-six minutes ago – and slash my own wrists in a cubicle. Of Kubrick's *2001: A Space Odyssey*, Ballard had written: 'its huge set pieces reminded me of *Gone with the Wind*, scientific pageants that became a kind of historical romance in reverse, a sealed world into which the hard light of contemporary reality was never allowed to penetrate.'* And the same could be said of any shopping mall worth its rental – and especially the Mall of the Emirates, where

---

* J. G. Ballard, *Crash* (1974), Introduction to the French edition.

PART OF THE LANDSCAPE.

the arches, embayment and balustrades insistently recalled to my mind episodes of *Star Trek*, wherein the crew of the USS *Enterprise* touch down on alien planets forever frozen in a 1960s evocation of the Italian Renaissance.

Downtown Dubai may have been U/C, but riding in my yellow Dubai taxi I was able to penetrate its bewildering defences – star-shaped roundabouts, concrete horn works, asphalt bastions – with disquieting ease. The core of this fortress comprises the Old Town, a purpose-built 'Arabian village', where – according to Emaar, the developer – 'you will live ensconced among these epochs while looking out at the very pinnacle of modernity'; to whit: the Burj. It's a vision thing, Dubai, and the very essence of Sheikh Mo's vision is its fecundity. Safi Qurashi, the owner of Great Britain Island, was to admonish me for not admiring the tremendous alacrity with which Sheikh Mo had scattered his magic seed, the rapidity of its germination, and the mighty pulsion with which these steely blooms had thrust skywards, but standing in front of the Palace Hotel – a massive reddish lump of Arabian Nights, complete with minarets, cusped arches, domed roofs and Kalasa finials – I could think only of Standard & Poor, who had downgraded Emaar's considerable debt from –A to BBB+. The developer had lost 1.6bn dirhams (£304m) in the last quarter of 2008, and however optimistic King Qurashi might be, Sheikh Mo's government had warned that the Dubai economy might well shrink in the second half of 2009.

Standard & Poor, and the almost indecent up-thrust of the big prick of the Burj, which poked the darkling empyrean beyond the Palace. Forgive me, Sigmund, for paraphrasing your apocrypha, but while sometimes a cigar may just be a cigar, a tall building is *always* a big dick – and what does it say of the Arabs that they feel compelled to erect so many of them? According to the CTBUH (Council on Tall Buildings and Urban Habitat), the acknowledged arbiter of loftiness, of the twenty tallest buildings in the world come 2020, 50 per cent will be in the Middle East, five of these will be in Dubai alone, and the Burj will be overlooked by the kilometre-high Nakheel Tower.

Probably no bad thing. The watchword of Adrian Smith, who designed the Burj for Skidmore Owings & Merrill (SOM), the US architectural practice, is 'contextualism', an alleged response to the rejection/evolution of big-bland-curtain-walled-box modernism. 'An architecture designed for war – on the unconscious level if no other'.* Some cynics I've spoken to have suggested that Smith's groundwork for his megaliths consists quite simply in 'walking around taking a few snaps', but in fairness to him, isn't this the true context of signature buildings such as the Burj? They are intended to be apprehended, fleetingly, on the screen of a digital camera, by Sansomite-baggers who will be gone in the morn – the fact that the Burj bears no relation to its context is a given: there is no fucking context. Before the contractors began work this site was an abandoned army camp on the desert fringes of the city, and now the Old Town Island has been 'created', the context for the Burj is a faux Islamic ville, its archways, porches, gardens, platforms and vistas – indeed, its entire spatial hierarchy – created from scratch. The Burj's 'Islamic' credentials rest on its triple-lobed floral floor plan, which is visible only from Sheikh Mo's helicopter, the building's own observatory, and possibly the Nakheel Tower.

I'm already feeling anxious about the Nakheel Tower – the sapping succubus of impotence wraps itself around Downtown Dubai's mighty loins. I'm worried about other erections in the Master Plan as well – what of HQ1, DS1, DS3, DS4, and my personal fave, FC2? What will any of us do without them? More specifically I'm concerned for the members of CTBUH, an organisation that, like SOM,

_____

70    *  J. G. Ballard, *High Rise*, (1975).

hails from Chicago. Are they feeling the wind of change in the windy city? Do they sit, futilely rubbing their crotches against the underside of their meeting-room table, knowing only too well that if others can't *get it up* they'll have nothing to do? For now, Emaar is keeping the erection-measurers in suspense, with no final decision on exactly how high the completed Burj will be – a mind-boggling foreplay as C80, the highest-strength concrete known to man (capable of withstanding 12,000 PSI gravity loads) is oh so delicately poured. Mmm.

Or maybe – I considered this after being offloaded at the Palace Hotel by the Swat man – Smith is in fact finely attuned to the very Bedouin functionalism that Thesiger identified, but rather than arranging three stones for a nomad's pot, for Sheikh Mo, Smith's arranging a gargantuan trilithon, the two uprights of which are the Burj Dubai and the Nakheel Tower? I shuddered to think what the cross-piece would look like, as I sauntered through the Palace's spotless lobbies with their alabaster bowls full of nothing, their winking tea lights and arrases behind which lurked the eunuchs of high finance. I stopped into the gift shop, and from pure reflex checked their map display – no sign of the elusive off-road Map 5, but there was a map of Dubai City printed on cloth. *Cloth?* What was I gonna do with that – surely only something that would lead me to fall foul of the proposed new media law, making it an offence to report gloomy economic news, such as: your city is covered in *snot*.

Outside, at the end of the pool, past the gleaming cabinet of shishas and the tented loungers, I took my place and sipped a ten quid tomato juice as the Burj wavered in the twilight. True, if you focused hard and concentrated on the fact that the derrick cranes near the building's summit must be ten storeys high, then the scale of the world's tallest building became apparent – but surely such an exalted edifice shouldn't require such an effort? *Squint upon my works, ye mighty* . . . I was waiting for my man – one of the team working on the Burj with responsibility for ensuring that the contractors fulfilled the design spec to the letter. He arrived looking cool, suited, booted – and in every way urbane. He ordered a Heineken, and when I remarked, 'Fuck Heineken,' he got the reference. Then he talked of step-backs and buttress cores, of how the asymmetric structure allowed for damping the inertia of the building's movement. He spoke of sputtering – the method used to coat the Burj's exterior cladding with the right synthetics to resist the climate. He expatiated on the relationship between the architects and Giorgio Armani, who would be responsible for some thirty-seven floors of hotel and a further sixty-four of apartments. My man seemed to feel that Armani embodied total design excellence – I thought only of his legendarily clean lines burning into my body: fiery brands – what could it be like to *live* inside a brand . . . ?

And what could it be like to live inside Armani himself? 'My clients,' he has said, 'come for me, they come back each season for my spirit.' So, let's get this straight: by buying an apartment designed by a 75-year-old workaholic, you would – in some strange sense – be *coming back* to him? Armani himself has admitted to spending a mere twenty nights in four years at a beautiful apartment that he owns facing on to Central Park in New York; so, in coming back to Armani, one is clearly not re-entering one's home – it might be better to regard the Armani apartment in the Burj as being on a par with a suit, merely one among a rack of apartments, slipped on for an evening, before being abandoned, crumpled, on the floor of the desert.

' . . . legacy projects.' My man was finishing saying something when I tuned back in, but then he added: 'I don't think that people here are any more opportunist than anyone else.' I looked at him blankly, trying to remember who he was, who I was, and what we were both doing here, sitting on a terrace in the Middle East looking at a Thai restaurant on the banks of an ornamental lake. 'People always ask how they get the last crane down,' *L'Uomo* Armani observed, mistaking my farsighted expression for Burj worship.

'Oh, I know already,' I said blithely. 'The workers disassemble it, then they cut it up with oxyacetylene torches, then they eat the bits of steel – I've seen them myself, squatting beneath the flyovers of the Sheikh Zayed Road, their faces a tormented rictus as they try to expel these evil shards.'

No, I didn't in fact say this, but I might as well have, for we were that far apart: he in his happy community – he had told me he lived out at the Marina, that he chatted with his neighbours – me with my vision of ruins to come:

'The high rise stank. None of the lavatories or garbage-disposal chutes were working, and a faint spray of urine hung over the face of the building, drifting across the tiers of balconies. Overlaying this characteristic odour, however, was a far more ambiguous smell, putrid and sweet, that tended to hover around empty apartments, and which Laing chose not to investigate too closely.'*

J. G. Ballard sited his fictional high rise on the Isle of Dogs; a decade later real high rises arose there, and Canary Wharf became the financial centre of London. One of the final components in the development – the completion of which had been

---

* J. G. Ballard, *High Rise*, (1975).

delayed by the recession of the early 1990s – was Canary Wharf Towers, topped out in 2001. The architect was Adrian Smith.

The cab driver who took me back to Deira, the old centre of Dubai City, was a young Pakistani man. I don't know if my questioning was a little brutal – how long have you been here? Where are you from? Is it OK, have you got enough money? – but after responding as best he could: nine months, Karachi . . . he stumbled over his third reply. Then, pulling up in front of the hotel, he put his fists in the inky shadows of his eye sockets. 'Life is bad,' he said simply.

London, April 2009

DUBAI-DUBAI-DOO !

# The Jeremiah Tree

Los Angeles, again. Sitting in the lobby of the Chateau Marmont on Sunset I listen idly to the beautiful native Angeleno as she tells me what she and her boyfriend – an equally beautiful Spaniard – did last New Year's Eve. 'We drove all the way out to the Joshua Tree man, and we did some 'shrooms and we just let it all sink in.'

'Yeah,' puts in the Spaniard, who's writing a doctoral thesis on deconstruction or construction – one or the other – 'and we made love, amazing, fragile love. It was too much in a way. Much too much. There were shooting stars, and these ancient trees, and the coyotes and bobcats . . . and, well . . . I felt a little, y'know . . . ' He laughs, embarrassed at his own psychic fragility, ' . . . like bits of me were dropping off.'

'I know what you mean.' I try and sound avuncular as I puff on my pipe, somewhere between a drug counsellor and a keen stamp collector. Yards of tweed pleat into hairy mountains in my crotch. However the tobacco I bought earlier in the day – Royal Vintage Matured Ribbon – is the rankest thing I've tasted since I last swigged a can of flat beer and fag butts, and the Angeleno is just a little too pulchritudinous for me to want to even *hear* that she's been making love, let alone imagine it taking place in the Mojave Desert. Bits of me are dropping off as well – and it isn't 'shrooms that are to blame.

Still, down in the hotel car park I have a sloppy General Motors coupé – a hire car for a hireling – and my flight out to London isn't until late the following afternoon; perhaps I too will head for the Joshua Tree and commune there under its giant toilet brush limbs? In fact – I must. Nothing hurts more than waiting in a vast and alien city for an intercontinental friction toy to whirr you into the stratosphere. The surly gravity of LA – pickled in its own nastiness of pollutants – drags you so that you feel like a grounded astronaut, each of your limbs subjected to 5gs of thrust, as you struggle to make it to the minibar for $6.50's worth of jellybeans.

Sunday morning, 7.30 a.m., and I swing out on to Sunset, my tyres squealing as they slap the oil-stained concrete. In LA it is pointless to adopt any psychogeographic perspective that is unmediated by the automobile. Don't walk or allow yourself to be driven, grasp the burning nettle of the twenty-first century and look at everything through a screen, or on one. This is not a city for the fainthearted or those who demand human scale, because it goes on and on and on. There are no featured players – only extras. By the time I reach the entrance ramp on to Highway 10 I feel as if I've done a good morning's driving. I listen to the Phil Collins station: WMCPHIL on the car radio, back-to-back plays of Phil's greatest hits, segued with advertisements for colonic irrigation and cryogenic preservation.

Chunk-a-clunka-chunk. Highway 10 rears and gallops through El Monte, Baldwin Park, West Covina, Pomona, Montclair, Ontario – the city is so big that it contains an entire fucking Canadian province within its boundless limits. Then around Banning on the edge of the desert it finally loses its grip, mountains rear up, eagles replace aerials. 'I can feel it coming in the air tonight . . . ' Phil expostulates, and I can only join in 'Oh Lord!' I pull in to a rest stop and stroll over to where an immaculate California Highway Patrol car idles; for several long moments I look at the two tousled mes in the mirrors of the patrolman's sunglasses, before asking how far it is to the turn off for the Park. 'Route 62 is about a half hour on, the Park entrance a half hour after that,' he replies unfazed; although I note that like all Americans he now pronounces 'route' to rhyme with 'doubt'.

This transformation occurred about ten years ago in a mass act of strange Stalinist forgetting on the part of the people. Now all Americans swear that they've always said 'rout' not 'root'. Even when you sing a few lines of 'Route 66' and point out to them that it isn't a song about the sixty-sixth time of putting an aggressor to flight, they still deny it. These things trouble me, trouble me more than the fat bourgeois weekender bikers who stream past me on the switchback road, more than the vast perimeter fence of the Twentynine Palms Marine Base to the north of the road, wherein a thousand thousand jarheads are ironing their hair before church.

By the time I reach the Park I have only half an hour to crunch the sand, climb a rounded rock, breathe the cool strained air, goggle at the leguminous toilet brushes. The Official Map and Guide is apologetic about the desert: 'Some think it wretched and seemingly useless', it says, as if describing a minor character in a play by Samuel Beckett. But it isn't the Park that's useless – it's me. I've driven for eight hours to take a half-hour walk. I thought I was rolling with the Firestone go-round of LA life, but really I'm just another piece of tousled roadkill.

# Plenty of Room in the Asylum

James Fox and I are in Calais; and for all I know now we will remain in Calais forever, entombed in its stony bosom, forever knocking on the solid shutters of its heart for admittance. The Hôtel de Ville may look like a Gothic enema pump, but what care I? Calais is quite French enough. Why, here we sit in a typical little café, the tables melamine, the walls deal-panelled, the ceiling nicotine-painted. So many shades of brown – it's enough to make me studious.

I've despatched James – who has superior language skills – to lock antlers with the *patron* concerning the fate of the notorious asylum seekers. These euphemisms have allegedly been clogging the streets of Calais since the British government forced the closure of the Sangatte detention centre, and I want to track them down. It was always an important part of the trip for me; we're in Calais for cheap fags – they're searching for a decent life; that these two quests should elide is psychogeography at its most poignant and hateful.

The *patron* joins us with a tourist map and begins to expatiate. James has no need to translate, for the fellow speaks the lingua franca of bigotry: 'All right,' he wheedles through his moustache 'granted the Italians are dodgy, and who gives a shit about the Americans, but it's up to us and the Germans – because we're basically sound. We should work together to send these scum back to where they come from. You're working men like me, you understand that they want our jobs, our homes, our wives even!'

'The *flics* have the right idea, they pick them up, drive them 200 kilometres inland and then dump them. But it's not far enough I tell you! They find their way back!'

'So where are they now?' we enquire like the decent working men we are. The *patron* turns his attention to the map and indicates the directions as if he were about to deploy a couple of nine-inch field guns to sort the problem out once and

WHO, IN THIS LIFE, IS NOT A REFUGEE FROM SOMEWHERE??

for all. We settle the tab and leave. '*Au revoir*' says the *patron* and I mutter, 'Yeah, like *jamais*.'

In the street we engage a taciturn cabbie who drives us across the Pont Georges and into the dock area. He gives us a more reasoned assessment of the situation: Yes, there are a few refugees, but mostly they've been dispersed among the other Channel ports. They're harassed by the police, they get nothing from the state, it's barely safe for them to be seen on the streets during the day. He pulls up under the searchlight beam of a brutal-looking lighthouse. There, in the porch of an ugly modernist church, we can see a huddle of asylum seekers, bodies like bedrolls, bedrolls like bodies.

It's them, the swarthy mob that are storming Fortress Europe, the southern horde that will topple our mighty government and pillage our great economy. There are about twenty of them in as many shades of white and brown and black. As we move towards them they come out from the shadows to meet us. James ends up talking to a young Sudanese in pidgin French, while I talk equally basic English with Florian, who's from near Budapest. Florian makes no pretension to persecution. In Romania he can make $100 a month fitting kitchens. Life is hard – and he's heard that there's a lot more money to be made in Britain. I concur wearily, thinking quite how much my own fitted kitchen set me back; looking round the shivering refugees a shadowy kitchen self-erects among them as if to taunt me. Florian is fatalistic: if he can't get to Britain he'll have to go home. It is as the *patron* and the cabbie say, life for the refugees in Calais is dreadful, and yes, the police do pick them up and dump them far inland. Only the Church allows them this mean sanctuary. James's Sudanese is in a worse position. He fled the civil war up country and because of his tribal affiliation he would be killed if he went back. He's no euphemism – he's the real thing.

Half an hour later we're sipping coffees in the well-appointed café-cum-shop of the Terminal Poids Lourds by the entrance to the Eurotunnel. It's here that refugees are meant to try and smuggle themselves into lorries bound for Britain, but there's no sign of them, just industrious security men checking semi-trailers. In the café the Beaujolais Nouveau *est arrivé*. We're offered a glass by the waitress, together with a little plate of *saucisson sec*. The French lorry drivers positively ooze well-unionised comfort; they are welcoming and emollient. Hell, I'm not surprised they're worried about having their jobs stolen by Sudanese asylum seekers – there's a couple of English journalists here who'd happily have them as well.

# Hermetic Wisdom

The hermit has always been an integral part of the landscaped garden. From its earliest inception, garden architects were encouraged to incorporate grottos into their picturesque evocations of the wild, and into these hermits were enticed, presumably with offers of a modest stipend. However, when no real hermit was forthcoming it was also perfectly acceptable to adopt a substitute. At the 'English' landscaped gardens of Forsmark in Sweden, the travel writer Linnerhielman found a grotto, with 'in its shadows a hermit, sitting with a book in his hand. He is dressed in a deep purple cloak, and has a gentle but serious expression. The figure was made of wax and later eaten by rats'.

Linnerhielman was writing in the late eighteenth century, but the hermit remains active (or should I say quiescent?) in the modern era. Looked at in one way, the roads protests of the 1990s were an attempt to halt the relentless autogeddon which is grinding the English countryside beneath its steely bulk; but from another angle I think it's clear that the protesters were hermits *manqués*, intent on seeking out trees and burrows within which they could contemplate the eternal verities, only to find themselves winkled out by temporary security operatives on the minimum wage.

During the protracted campaign waged to prevent the construction of the Newbury bypass, I found myself deep in conversation with a beardie dubbed Balon who'd suspended himself in a kind of sling dangling from a tripod of twenty-foot-long scaffolding poles. Doubtless Balon considered himself to be in Middle Earth as much as Middle England, yet there was something altogether touching about his literal suspension of disbelief, poised as his tripod was on the ratty verge alongside the B1562.

The hermit who most influenced my own life was called Peter Buxton. He lived in a curious hut which adjoined the even more curious cottage of an old friend of

my father's in a Suffolk seaside village. Creek Cottage was a series of ramshackle wooden extensions bolted on to an inner sanctum of ordinary brickwork. In the extensions bunk beds were fabricated at odd angles and inappropriate heights, many of them furnished with their own bookshelves and plant boxes. You could lie all day under an exploding eiderdown, reading Charlie Chaplin's autobiography and listening to the creak of weatherboarding, while the tendrils of a spider plant tickled your nose. Or else venture outside into a soused world of salt-water creeks, reed beds and sand dunes, with a derelict windmill in the mid-distance signalling the victory of the elements.

The story was (and I have no idea whether or not it was apocryphal) that Peter had once been an architect at the old London County Council, and that in this capacity he was responsible for much of the high-rise dehumanisation of the East End. Eventually, driven by his conscience, Peter had a kind of epiphanic breakdown, and became a hermit. I have to say that as hermits go Peter Buxton was, to my way of thinking, the real thing. Long and straggly of beard and hair, face nut-brown and weatherbeaten, clothing a tatter-medallion of trouser, string and Wellington boot. He cultivated an allotment, looked after the cottage, and sat in his hut, where on smooth floorboards he read sutras in front of a single nightlight.

When staying at the cottage I'd join him there, sit cross-legged opposite him, receive cups of herbal tea or vegetable soup, and indulge in very quiet conversations, in the course of which – if my memory serves me right – he would retail gentle spiritual counsel. Even more significant though was the occasion when I came off a moped a bunch of us were larking about with on one of the stony tracks which wended down to the beach. The graze festered and then the arm began to swell. Eventually, in considerable pain, I went to consult Peter, who without demur lashed a bundle of herbage to the purulent sore. To my considerable surprise – and relief – when I woke the next morning all the pus had been leached from the wound. Now, that's what I call a hermit.

Creek Cottage's eccentric owner died a long time ago, and Peter Buxton died not long after. Some say he was a victim of prospective rehousing, that he starved himself to death rather than be uprooted from his grotto. Certainly, it was as difficult to imagine him separated from his hut, as it was to conceive of him as a thrusting champion of 1960s Modernism. If I ever visit the village now I always walk along the sea wall and take a look at the cottage, half hoping that it's reverted to its 1970s state of ramshackle recklessness, but no, the place is now as tidy and foursquare as any Barratt Home, while even the waxwork of its hermit has been eaten away at by the rodents of time.

# Sodom Bypass

It's difficult to imagine the point at which you would begin to find the road sign 'Sodom 60 kilometres' unremarkable – let alone banal. Still, I suppose if you drive the road out of Jerusalem and down towards the Dead Sea enough times in your life, the decision on whether to turn left ('Jericho 10 kilometres'), or right – to the aforementioned Sodom – will be dictated by purely prosaic considerations. 'Oh, I always do the food shopping in Sodom,' you might be subject to saying, or 'Got to go, I have to get the kids from school in Jericho' could spring from your lips, equally unbidden. It would be nice to think that these resonant names, encrusted with the most ancient and powerful of associations, were nonetheless being smoothed by the stream of time and usage, to become merely quotidian pebbles.

Nice but untrue. Far from the supplanting of one Palestinian population by another burying these place names in semantic sands, the ingathering of the Jews has infested them with new and troubling vigour. Over two hundred years of rigorous biblical scholarship and increasingly scientific archaeology, rather than demoting Bethlehem, Nazareth, Beersheeba et al. from their quasi-mystical status, have instead invested them with still more messianic fervour.

Of course, disputing the ownership of a place is bound to make its name resound. In his great anecdote 'The Night the Bed Fell', James Thurber recounted how, while lying in bed one night, he found himself repeating the place name 'Perth Amboy' (a town in New Jersey), over and over again until the syllables began to have no meaning whatsoever; worse, Thurber felt himself being sucked into a vortex of meaninglessness as the world was voided of its referents. You can try the reverse thought experiment for yourself by imagining that the place where you live is the flashpoint for the Third World War. Picture the headlines of newspapers: 'Army Moves into Little Snoring'; 'Ethnic Cleansing in Little Snoring'; 'Chemical Weapons Used on Little Snoring Village Hall'; visualise the howling populace, the snarling soldiery, the canting politicos. Before too long I'm pretty sure the words 'Little Snoring' will become synonymous in your mind with Iwo Jima, or Sarajevo, or Golgotha for that matter.

On my sole trip – so far – to Israel, I visited quite a few of those resounding places and even took a dip in the Dead Sea. This latter activity I cannot warn you against too strenuously. True, any reasonably sane person understands that such saline fluid is bound to sting and smart if you have the slightest abrasion or cut anywhere on your body, but what I didn't reckon on was that this minatory pond (because, let's face it, how can a sea be below sea level?), would even manage to *create* new fissures in my skin and reduce me to a stinging, whimpering wreck. Buoyed up on a Lilo of pain, I stared up at the escarpment to the west, where the zealous Maccabees held out against the Roman legions, until, maddened by starvation, they committed mass suicide.

It occurred to me that those of us who live still further to the west misunderstand

the countervailing pressures on contemporary Israeli society. On the one hand you have the fundamentalists, who in seeking to establish a vast Eretz Israel rely on a bowdlerised version of their own history, cooked up by priests in the seventh-century BCE court of King Joshua; while on the other you have the secularists, who are intent on founding a kind of *über*-Milton Keynes, complete with Judea Crescents and Samaria Avenues. The Israeli settlements in the *soi-disant* Occupied Territories are merely the outposts of this troubling exercise in garden city planning.

Neither approach has anything to offer the Palestinians, whose own, few remaining place names have become synonymous with pain, dispossession and state-sanctioned murder. Deprived of a nation of their own, these people are reduced to residing in a 'strip' and a 'zone', scrag ends of territory chopped off from the body politic. It's very hard to imagine these Emmenthal cities, bored through again and again by bulldozers, artillery shells and mortars, becoming merrily commonplace: 'It's showing at the multiplex in Ramalah', or 'I think they've got potting soil at the Jenin garden centre', are not phrases that it's easy to form, even as thought experiments.

Notoriously credulous visitors to the Holy Land are afflicted with 'Jerusalem Syndrome'. Overawed to be walking the self-same cobbles as Lord Jesus, they fall victim to the delusion that they too are anointed, and have to be hauled off to the local psych ward for a generous shot of Thorazine. I myself suffered the exact reverse of this affliction, finding such sacrosanct sites as the Wailing Wall and the Via Dolorosa to be respectively: a large pile of breeze blocks and a rather smelly alley. It was while musing on all of this that I found my bus passing a sign which read 'Sodom 5 kilometres', pointing back the way we'd come. Damn it! After all that I'd missed the place – presumably there was a bypass.

# The Carpet Moves

I've been in minor earthquakes a couple of times in my wandering life. The first was in 1983, I was working in Darwin for the Lands Department of the Northern Territory of Australia. My dad had fixed this up for me, and with the true fervour of the remittance man I'd gone after it like a greyhound chasing a lure. I'd pitched up in Canberra – where Dad lived – on the run from my bad habits in London, but strange to tell I soon managed to track down plenty of ne'er-do-wells in this idealised garden city of a capital. Surely, I reasoned, Darwin would be far enough from anywhere for me to avoid serious trouble?

A lot of other addicts *manqués* had had exactly the same idea, and I soon fell in with them. We slaked our thirst for intoxication with six-packs of Emu Export and bushels of domestic weed. It was a decade after the hurricane which had devastated Darwin, and the town was still clambering back up from its knees to its feet. Along with people on the run from the southern cities, the gaff was full of civil servants on padded salaries, egregious rednecks in from the sticks, and enigmatic aboriginals who sat in tousled groups under the thick tropical foliage on the median strips of the town's sleepy boulevards.

My job was to assess the demand for building land in the Northern Territory. This was not exactly scarce, given that it's six times the size of the British Isles, and the population was then under 100,000. A cursory examination of the stats told me that the population – and hence the rate of household formation – rose and fell in line with the federal subsidy, my report could've consisted of this sentence alone. However, I was drawing a generous salary for a four-month contract – why rock the boat. My nominal boss seldom appeared in the office, preferring to pathway plan his yacht, or play at being the Austrian Consul, a comic operetta role for which there was no more requirement than his laughable services as an economist.

I began attending the office with Proustian legerdemain, preferring to spend most of my time in the Swan Hotel reading *À la recherche du temps perdu*, and downing stubbie after stubbie. So it was quite by chance that I happened to be

on the sixth floor of the government building – which was at that time the highest thing in Darwin after the casino – when a scale 6 earthquake burbled up from the bed of the Arafura Sea some five hundred miles to the north-east. The white

walls supporting the Sasco Year Planner bulged, the vertical textured louvres riffled, we shirt-sleeves headed as one for the emergency stairs.

In the street I was astonished to see the roadway, the pavement, the verges, all undulate as if they were a giant carpet runner being yanked at one end. Visible waves moved through the solid earth, lifting the gaggle of guvvie workers up and down as if we were surfers waiting in the swell to catch a big one. The quake can't have lasted for more than four or five minutes, but it was long enough for me to recoil from the complete transmogrification of matter. Land shouldn't 'quake' – or undulate for that matter. Land should sit there, the prosaic basis of all that is, rigidly and uncompromisingly supporting the leisurely lifestyles of types like me, just as it supports Ayers Rock, or the Parthenon for that matter. If earth was going to quake, then what next? Locust plagues? Parting watercourses? Or would the air turn into a crystal and suffocate us all in its infinite refractions?

But the most peculiar thing about the quake was the response of some Tiwi Islanders who formed the extended family of one of my most eccentric colleagues. John, a native East Ender, had arrived in Australia in the 1960s, after riding a moped most of the way there despite being crippled by polio. He was pretty much shunned by the rest of the Department because he chose to hang out with the blackfellers. The contrast between small, white, bespectacled, balding John, and the magnificently tall and shaggy-haired Tiwi Islanders (who are really the Watusi of Native Australians), was something to behold. A couple of nights after the quake I was hanging out with them all when some of the Tiwis became agitated for no reason I could discern. When I asked John what was going on he said: 'They've just heard some of their people were killed on Cape York during the quake.'

'Heard?' I queried. 'Heard how?'

'Oh, the usual way,' he grinned, 'meaning not by phone.'

It was all of a piece: the satirical statistical job, the liquefying earth, and the telepathic trunk calls that took two days to place. It was with some relief that I returned to the Boulevard St Germain.

# No Country
# for Wise Men

My column about Peter Buxton, the hermit I knew when I was a lad (see Hermetic Wisdom, p. 83), garnered a massive postbag. By 'massive' I mean five letters, but frankly when it comes to writing about the relationship between topography and the psyche that's effectively a papery deluge.

To recap, when I knew him in the 1970s Peter Buxton was the resident hermit of a ramshackle and bohemian cottage in a seaside Suffolk village owned by an eccentric elderly lady, Francesca Wilson. But it was said that Peter was formerly an architect at the London County Council, and had been responsible for much of the high-rise dehumanisation of the East End. Apparently, he had a kind of breakdown of conscience and then became a hermit of the classic type: reading sutras, humming ragas, eating brown rice and applying herbal poultices.

All of my correspondents had known Peter personally and added to my recollections. Val Cloake of Hanwell limned in the hermit's arrival: 'The story was that the price Francesca had paid for Creek Cottage included Peter. He had helped her turn it into the hostel I knew. He also built a rather lovely shed in the garden for himself, before that he had lived in a packing case in the garden. He kept the packing case, complete with curtains and bookshelves, for times when the house was full, then he would move out of his shed and back into the packing case. This was long and narrow and he could just slide down inside it. He could even lie in it and read with the help of a nightlight. He seemed to have little need of softness or comfort. At one point Francesca received a letter from the local authority enquiring whether she was aware that she had a man living in a packing case in her garden. It really isn't the kind of thing that escapes your attention, is it?'

Lewis Kinnear of Dumfries had a different angle on this peculiar domicile: '. . . he'd had some sort of nervous breakdown which resulted in his ending up on the beach at Walberswick. Francesca Wilson had found him living in an old

Peter Buxton · MK 2 · Artist · Architect · Visionary · Hermit · Loser    Ralph Steadman 2004

piano packing case which had washed up on the beach.' But it was Robin Kirton of Newdigate, Surrey, who had the strongest reaction to the original piece, and the most poignant information to impart.

He wrote: 'I read with mounting astonishment mixed with regret your column in the *Independent* magazine of 14th February on the subject of hermits. Peter Buxton was a close friend and colleague in the Architects Department of the LCC. In many ways his experiences there were even less happy than the apocryphal account you have been given.' I read Mr Kirton's letter with mounting astonishment as well, for here was the truth about a long-dead hermit. I learned from Mr Kirton's eloquent and comprehensive account that Peter Buxton had been employed in the General rather than the Housing Division of the Department. He was not – so far as my correspondent knew – responsible for designing high rises.

Peter Buxton did however fall foul of the Department, when, bucking the prevailing tendency to build vast and soulless old people's homes, he designed 'a truly brilliant scheme' for a home off Brixton Hill. On the scale of a traditional almshouse, the home featured self-contained bedsitting room units ranged around small courts. 'Peter was a fine artist and his drawings were utterly seductive', so despite its conflict with the orthodox brief, his home got built. However 'hardly surprisingly it went well over budget because Peter was absolutely meticulous in his detailing and demanded and got good workmanship'. It was after this that Peter Buxton was transferred to the Housing Division.

Mr Kirton continued: 'Whilst I was away on leave Peter literally vanished. He had a bedsit near Kew Gardens where he had entertained my wife and myself . . . It was a room at the top of a large Victorian house with sloping ceilings and complex attic spaces. He lived at floor level on cushions surrounded by books and his then huge LP collection. His cooking was miraculous despite the minimal means at his disposal. It was my introduction to mint tea and strange cheeses. On the last time we visited he lent me the Klemperer recording of Beethoven's 9th. Because even his delightful landlord either didn't know, or was forbidden to tell me where he had gone, we thought he had gone to Devon – he had said his mother lived in that part of the country.'

This, then, was the backstory of the benevolent and big-bearded man who had cured my infected elbow when I fell off my moped. Who drank mint tea with me too, while trying to talk some calm into my fevered adolescent brow. I don't know which part of the tale is the more poignant – but at least now it has a beginning as well as an end.

# Gayvaria

I always feel just a little bit gay when I'm in Germany, it's probably a way of dodging the fact that I'm half-Jewish. It's an old sawhorse for Jews travelling to present-day Germany, but it does take a good few visits before the horripilation dies down, and you don't feel the whistling of a – figurative – axe, about to descend on the nape of your neck. Walter Abish, the great Austrian Jewish novelist summed it up in *How German Is It?* The protagonist of this tale returns to an unnamed town that he lived in before the Holocaust. Looking at the local map outside the station, he becomes transfixed by the very Germanness of it, the sheer fact that every little rivet, every wire graticule, is German right down to its atoms, and that – preposterously – He Is There.

Well, I've travelled to Germany a fair bit in the last decade, and with each successive visit, marked only by kindness, civility and aching formality on the part of my hosts, the Germanness of it has ceased to be quite so *unheimliche*. I've stayed in kitsch hotels in Berlin with glass engraved doors, lacy pillowcases and sportive putti on the ceiling rose; and hung out at minimalist ones in Munich. At the Hopper Hotel I asked which one it was named after, Dennis or Edward? The desk clerk thought for a while, before answering thoughtfully: 'Both, I think.' I've marvelled at the colonic terror inspired in me by the sight of the mighty, calcified spire of Cologne Cathedral, and I've given many many literary readings.

Readings in which the German version of my text has been declaimed by – among others – a famous classical actress (Hamburg); a woman who does a hit TV show with a chimpanzee sidekick (Hanover); and an orotund chain-smoking literary critic (Berlin). This last outing, at the Literarisches Colloquium, is where I'm aiming for, but first the matter of my German gayness.

Arriving a couple of years ago in Munich, I found myself settling into the Hotel Olympic on Hans Sachs Strasse with great ease. The staff were all very friendly,

neat-looking young men. Right next door there was a café-bistro, where the barmen and the patrons were all very friendly, neat-looking young men. Wandering the streets I encountered many finely turned out young Bavarian men in tight, tight lederhosen and immaculate loden jackets. I remarked on all of this to my publicist, Martin. 'Oh yes,' he replied in faultless English, 'we call this part of town "Gayvaria".' I liked Gayvaria just fine, but I couldn't ascertain whether its gayness vitiated or enhanced the How-German-Is-It effect. Did I feel better there because we were all in it together? Or was it that a certain camp quality is intrinsic in German militarism, so that its gayness was merely of a piece?

The next day we entrained for Hanover, where I found myself giving a seminar in a very hot room on the top floor of the Brutalist university. Over the roofs of the city lowered three, enormous, gently belching power station chimneys. 'They're quite something,' I remarked to Martin. He smiled quizzically and laid a hand on my arm. 'Yes,' he replied, 'in Hanover they're known as the "warm Brüder". It's a pun you see, because this is also slang for a –'

'Yes, yes, I know,' I beat him to it, 'a homosexual.'

'Quite so.'

Two days later we were in Berlin. I usually travel alone on book tours, so as not to succumb to the drone-like feeling which comes with having all your arrangements made for you. But Martin was not to be shaken, and so effective was he that I'd long since relapsed into a semi-comatose state, allowing Germany to become a species of wallpaper spooling past my tired eyes. There was this soporific, and there were also the continual discussions on arcane aspects of linguistic philosophy. In Germany almost everyone under the age of thirty-five is writing a thesis on Schlick, Jaspers or the Vienna Circle. Martin, being a bit of a rebel, was doing his on Theodor Adorno.

So immersed were we in the jargon of authenticity, that I didn't realise where we were until the cab pulled up in a street lined by opulent mansions, and through a break in the trees I saw the bright blue waters of a large lake. 'Blimey!' I expostulated, 'This is . . . this is Wannsee, isn't it.'

'That's right,' Martin was imperturbable, 'and that's the Literarisches Colloquium right over there.'

'But this is . . . this is where the Nazis planned the –'

'The Final Solution, quite correct. The house where they held the conference is there, across the lake. I think you'll find that it's now a rather excellent museum.'

I felt a surge of gayness and pushed Martin hard on his Frankfurt School shoulder. 'Get away with you!' I cried.

# Battersea!

We had a massive geography teacher when I was in my early teens, and by massive I mean physically huge. I've got some kind of a mental block about his name, probably because we were cruel to the poor fellow in a way that only thirty thirteen-year-olds can be: ritualistically, gleefully, unstintingly, acting with the unfettered sadism of many concentration camp guards with but a single inmate.

The exchange between Mr Wells (I'll call him this for convenience) and our class, which sealed for ever his status as a hapless butt, occurred when he asked us to 'Name a power station – any power station.' There was a slight fermata in the usual brouhaha and then we got back to being disruptive. 'Go on!' Mr Wells was reduced to bellowing. 'Name a power station! ANY POWER STATION!' A hand went obliquely up towards the back of the class; it was Sid Gold, a dreadful wiseacre who already had an account at the bookie's, and who bought Parma ham at the Italian deli during lunch break, then skipped around in the street cawing: 'Where's the rabbi now!' If Gold had put up his hand it's because he believed he had newly minted coinage of great wit. 'Yes Gold,' Mr Wells ventured with some trepidation 'can *you* name a power station?'

'Battersea sir, Battersea Power Station.'

'Yes, Battersea,' Wells's solid bar of brown moustache crinkled with approbation, 'good man Gold, good man.'

That did it for us, for the balance of school years whenever we saw poor Wells come looming down the corridor we would poke our evil little fingers in his direction and crow, 'Yes, Battersea, good man, good man!' before collapsing into helpless giggles. Why exactly we should have found this quite as amusing as we did remains utterly beyond me. I would say: you had to be there, but I was there, and still don't know. Perhaps it was because the great salience of Battersea Power Station on the London skyline made its naming a statement of the ludicrously obvious; or

TEACHER

maybe it was because both Wells and the Power Station, were seriously out of scale.

Wells wasn't the only Brobdingnagian geography teacher on the premises, there were Messrs Purves and Hinchcliffe as well. All three exceeded six foot four, and all three were alumni of Loughborough Polytechnic where they'd studied the academic equivalent of chewing gum and walking at the same time: Geography and PE. But while Wells had a 'tache, a perm and an equine face bridled with anxiety, Purves sported a devilish ginger beard and the chiselled good looks one associates with neoclassical sculptures of the Ancient Greek pantheon. Purves brooked no backchat and could rain down thunderbolts from his Olympian perspective. He was the first man I ever saw wear a tracksuit in the street – clearly it was the Shapelessness of Things to Come. As for Hinchcliffe, he was of an extreme height – perhaps seven foot – and very sadly died of heart failure when I was in the lower sixth. The school, being of almost celestial crumminess, memorialised him in the library with a small sign affixed to a shelf of geography text books which proclaimed: 'The Brian Hinchcliff Memorial Shelf'.

I wish I could tell you that despite all of this my geography lessons planted in me a seed of interest which over the decades grew into the mighty psychogeographical redwood you see before you. But I can't. Apart from the Battersea anecdote and a desultory field trip to somewhere near Luton where we observed synclines and anticlines, I can recall next to nothing of those millennia of sodden Thursday afternoon double periods. I wonder if anyone can? People are always claiming to have had inspired pedagogues – but very few of them seem to have been geographers.

No, my own interest in the perplexing polarity of topography and its representation derives – as so much has – from my father. Dad, as regular readers of this column will know, not only was an academic who specialised in urban development, but also had little or no personal modesty. Many was the time as a lad, that I would blunder into the toilet and find my father, squatting there like an old bull over his own dung, and with a map spread over his knees. The varicose veins on his spindly shanks seemed to segue with whorls of contour lines which indicated the height of the South Downs or the Black Mountains.

Yes, the Ordnance Survey was Dad's laxative easeful reading. He actually preferred to examine old maps – the kind printed on paper backed with linen – when at stool. At the time I found this as risible as Mr Wells, but with the benefit of hindsight I can see that Dad preferred to psychically perambulate in a pre-First World War Arcadia, long before Battersea Power Station or Loughborough Polytechnic reared their ugly heads.

# The Crayfish Quadrille

My mate Jamie says he's driven to the moon in his beaten-up old Renault van. I take this claim with a whole packet of Maldon sea salt (which, as any gourmand knows, is revered for its distinctively 'salty' taste), but there's no disputing the fact that he's done a lot of driving. The old van had clocked up 150,000 miles and the new one was nearing 100,000 before he'd finally had enough. Enough of delivering shapeless parcels to shadowy businesses in Corby, Telford and Basingstoke; enough of grinding down the blacktop for service centre after service centre; enough, in short, of passing life by.

One day, maddened by inertia, Jamie parked up the van and lunging through the overgrown verge found himself on the banks of a stream. He got into conversation with a bloke who was ambling about and talk turned to fishing – which Jamie is keen on. It transpired that the ambler was in possession of a stretch of the Thames bank outside Oxford and wanted to rent the fishing rights for fifty quid a year. Visions not just of hooking monstrous barbel, but also of being able to say 'I have some fishing rights up in Oxfordshire . . .' spurred our man on – and he cut a deal there and then. However, when he took possession of his stretch, instead of hooking chub and trout, on the end of his line were feisty little crustaceans.

Crayfish to be precise. American crayfish. Mississippi Delta crayfish sucked up into the ballast tanks of oceangoing freighters, then purged into the treacly waters of the Thames Estuary. For the past couple of decades these involuntary economic migrants have been sneaking up our sludgy byways, slowly but steadily infiltrating the entire river system of south-east England. They eliminate our native crayfish; vermiculate our river banks; gobble up aquatic plants and fish eggs; in short, do everything they can to de-oxygenate the water, making it fit only for themselves. Bastards. However, in their defence, they are right tasty – heavier, denser and gamier than langoustine, with a certain muddy piquancy.

CRAYFISH QUADRILLE

Jamie certainly thought so once he'd boiled a few alive and snaffled their tails. He also discovered that there was a market for crayfish up in the Smoke. With the dreamlike clarity of El Dorado glimpsed through a pass between mountains of shit, Jamie saw a permanent way out of the van. He obtained a licence from the Environment Agency to rid twenty miles of the Thames from this troublesome plague; he obtained orders from restaurateurs of his acquaintance. He went down river – way down river to the mudflats of South Benfleet, where he maxed out his plastic on a twenty-five-foot cruiser, the *Alberta*; and a little launch – *Petulance*.

Anchored out in the middle of the estuary in stygian darkness, awaiting the dawn and the flood tide, while multi-storey tankers cut upstream towards Gravesend and Tilbury, Jamie had understandable misgivings. Here he was, a native Londoner, for the first time ever without a home in the capital, and about to be washed into the Heart of England. It was a leave-taking worthy of some latter-day Catherine Cookson heroine, and as God turned up the contrast knob, and the *Alberta* swung about, Jamie vowed to do his best. Gargled upriver and through the humungous, steely bracelet of the Thames Barrier, ingurgitated by the Pool of London, gulped up by Teddington Lock, the cockleshell at last arrived on the banks of Port Meadow outside Oxford; where, since time immemorial, dozy cattle have cropped the sward while dozy students crop the 'shrooms.

Oxford has always been a magnet for travellers – whether by road or river. Although the colleges no longer dispense alms, the psyches of water gypsies and new-agers alike are ingrained with ancient folkways. There's a peculiar feeling I always get, looking at the sterns of the polyglot vessels moored along the bank where the river crosses under the ring road, that *Avaricious*, *Dandelion Clock*, *Sportive* and *Catalina* are about to cast off and head for the Preselli Mountains, where they'll load up with bluestones in order to construct a Modernist henge.

Needless to say, Jamie has fitted right into this community. He's made friends with a hairy narrowboatman, and together they set the traps out each evening, every one baited with a third of a chicken leg and smeared with cod liver oil. Mmm! Such are the Environment Agency's rules that they have to stay in the vicinity of the traps all night, which they do, sleeping under a tarp in *Petulance*. Then, at dawn, up come the crayfish, and for a few short hours they slumber under their trapper's watchful eye. Then it's into the van and down to St John or The Admiralty, or any one of an increasing number of eateries where you can simultaneously gratify your need to preserve the environment and your taste buds. It definitely beats driving to the moon when it comes to reducing emissions.

# Captain Birdseye

The Black-backed Gull is a most curious animal, it's what zoologists call a 'ring species', populations are found right around the world in a continuous band. Black-backs on this side of the globe can, of course, mate successfully; they can also mate successfully with Black-backs a few degrees further on, and those gulls can in turn mate with their neighbours. However, 'our' Black-backs cannot mate with Black-backs on the far side of the world. Cursed gull! Why must you taunt us with your giddy global go-round of copulation?

Yes, it's the gull that troubles me – not the ins and outs of evolution by natural selection. To be frank, I don't like gulls, I don't like their yellow eyes, their monocular stare, their thermal posturing – the way they insist on *hanging about*. My idea of hell would've been to be marooned on St Kilda, when that remote Hebridean island was still utterly dependent on seafowl. The St Kildans ate puffins, gannets and fulmars. They exported their feathers, they used gannet corpses as shoes (I kid you not), and anointed the umbilicuses of their newborn babies with fulmar oil; a practice which, by introducing tetanus, greatly increased infant mortalities and led – some believe – to the eventual evacuation of the island in the 1930s.

It was all perfectly all right when gulls kept to their places. If you go walking along the high sea cliffs of the British Isles you can reasonably expect to run across a few thousand gulls. Likewise, if you pitch up in any seaside town the world over, the presence of a gull, standing on a rooftop opposite your hotel window and waiting for you to go out and buy some chips, is a reasonable accompaniment to the whole *à la plage* experience. But that wasn't enough for the gulls – oh no. It's as if they've spent the last half century or so watching Hitchcock's *The Birds* over and over again, before finally deciding to cash in on film stardom with a few personal appearances.

Nowadays you can see gulls opening supermarkets in the middle of England at

SHARGH

SHI TURKISH SEAGULLS ARE E

any time of the year. 'Look,' I often say to these narcissistic fowl, 'you are *sea*gulls, get it?' They never deign to answer, save with their high-pitched yelping, which sounds like fingernails scraping the blue board of the sky. Supermarkets, town centres, landfill sites in the East Midlands, the playing fields of our most select public schools – there is nowhere sufficiently urbane, or far enough away from the briny, that the gulls don't consider it a reasonable habitat. A few nights ago I saw a common gull proceeding along the South Lambeth Road with great insouciance – and riding a fox.

The truth is I do understand the reason for this horrific *bouleversé* – we have only ourselves to blame. We've screwed up their habitat, while leaving large quantities of edible muck lying around ours. You can hardly blame a bird for opportunism. So why this Self–gull antagonism? Well, it goes back to the sojourn I had some years ago on the Shetland island of Unst. I put up with the Laird, whose reduced circumstances meant that he and the Lairdess were operating a B&B. It being midsummer I resolved to walk in the midnight sun of those parts, to the uttermost point of Britain, a cape called Hermaness.

Now, it happened that the Laird's grandfather, a keen ornithologist, had been responsible for the preservation of the Great Skua, a gull known colloquially – for reasons that will become apparent – as the bonxie. These bonxies were encouraged to breed on Hermaness, and breed they did. They are large, brownish birds, aggressively territorial, and with the rather alarming habit of dive-bombing the heads of any humans who venture too close to their nests. As I slogged up on to the top of the ness the first bonxie lifted lazily up off its nesting site and came swooping down towards me. If it hadn't been for a convenient stick which I was able to whirr about my head, my eyeball would have ended up as a beak ornament – or so I suspected.

I couldn't prevent a tremendous howl of fear and rage: 'Fucking bonxies!' Whereupon about sixty more took to the air. The next two hours were a vigorous workout for arms as well as legs, as skua after skua made its run. When I got back to civilisation some wiseacre told me all you have to do to stop the bonxies hitting you is wear a bobble hat, because they always aim for the highest point. Still, I wasn't to know this – any more than the foul fowl were to know that I'd no sooner eat their offspring than . . . err, eat their offspring.

# Small is Beautiful

Surrey, summer 2005. In Painshill Park, a kidney-shaped expanse of eighteenth-century, landscaped gardens, marooned in the tarmac oxbow of the M25, grown men are floating on an ornamental lake. I must qualify this statement: the men are not floating as swimmers float, but patrolling the inland sea inside scale models of First World War-era dreadnoughts. At least, that's what the warships look like to me, I'm no expert. Besides, the juxtaposition between the model and the ornamental is so deranging that – especially when one of the men opens the deck of his ship and his gargantuan bonce emerges above the thwarts – I suspect I may be having an acid flashback.

Why is it that we, as a people, are so instinctively drawn to the miniature? The landscaped garden is itself a form of stunted terrain, with mounds and dells contrived so as to give the carefully positioned viewer awesome prospects of distant hills and plunging dales. When the eighteenth-century Romantics conceived the notion of the sublime, they had merely trotted a few miles away from twee Southern England and into the terrible wastes of . . . Wales. It was adjudged a far wiser thing for gentlefolk to have diminutive recreations of the sublime contrived, than venture – like those daredevils Coleridge and De Quincey – into the wild crags of the Lake District.

Or take the grotto, a form of landscaped garden furniture that became so popular there were specialised companies dedicated to their production. Painshill has one of the finest grottos in England, and when we visited it was being painstakingly restored with crystalline chunks cemented to its vaulted roof. As I stared out through a knobbly embrasure, I could almost imagine that I were in a great, subterranean cavern, were it not for the ditsy dreadnought which hove into view. Or take the rage for rock gardening which got going in the nineteenth century. In part this was a quite reasonable desire to introduce mountain species into the low-lying

English garden, but as the rock piles towered higher and higher, becoming increasingly gnarled and baroque, so the Himalaya itself was cut down to size.

Lévi-Strauss sagely remarked that when we alter scale we 'sacrifice the sensible in favour of the intelligible'. Tell that to the Hampshire Model Boat Society, with their mini-dreadnoughts. Actually, I wouldn't mind telling them – because it's one thing to be the sort of saddo who labours in the privacy of his shed to produce a teensy simulacrum of a dreadful war machine, it's quite another to load it on a trailer, drag it up the M3 and go cruising. I'm confident that the kind of chap who could conceive of such a recreation is fully attuned to its warped heuristics.

As it is to the bucolic – so it is to the urban. I have visited most of Britain's principal cities and they have much to recommend them, from the austere pinkish granite of Aberdeen to the dinky lanes of Truro, with its disproportionately (there I go again) massive cathedral towering above them. Yet the town I return to again and again is about 1/30th actual size. Bekonscot Model Village may not be Britain's largest example of miniaturism – that accolade, I fear, must belong to Legoland – but it does have the virtue of being satisfyingly a world entire. Albeit a world mired in the inter-war period – for Bekonscot is the littlest of Little England, complete with churches, greens, castles and cottage hospitals. The harvest is threshed with steam power, there is an extensive, pre-Beeching rail network, and although in recent years ethnic minority figurines have been introduced, they look slightly anachronistic next to a fully functioning, nationalised mine.

The model village is set in the heart of Beaconsfield and advertised by large, steel signs along the M40, which, were they to fall on top of it, would destroy a large proportion of the housing stock. This isn't the only confrontation between the sensible and the intelligible that Bekonscot affords. To walk its narrow paths in the company of a huddled queue of Pantagruels is to be continually reminded of the sublime: will that hundred-foot-high toddler run amok and destroy the aerodrome? Will that goldfish – the size of a killer whale – capsize those doughty canoeists? Sadly there aren't any dreadnoughts full of enthusiastic modellers patrolling the pocket ocean of Bekonscot – but then you can't have everything.

If only everyone would embrace my own enthusiasm for microgeography! The spoilation of our towns and cities is a lot easier to contemplate through the wrong end of a telescope. Take wind farms; I can sympathise with those who view them as a grotesque imposition, however, if we picture these novelty windmills as just that: children's beach toys buried in the sward, and the countryside itself as a counterpane land, then global warming will, undoubtedly, become a lot more bearable.

# Agoraphobia

I once asked my mother what were the most significant changes she had noticed in London since she arrived in the late 1950s. She answered in a flash: 'There was one restaurant in Hampstead, and when you wanted to go somewhere by car, whether it was the Tate Gallery or the US Embassy – you drove there, parked outside and walked in.' I was mightily impressed by this answer; it demonstrated that my mother was on top of things, hanging ten on the breaking wave of the Zeitgeist.

Yet despite having upped sticks, and dragging her 11-year-old son with her to another country, Mother was not a doughty traveller. She journeyed, certainly, but always under some duress. Even as a child I got the distinct impression that while she couldn't bear being cooped up at home, going outside was another kind of torment. When I grew older the reason for this became clear: I discovered that she had suffered throughout her adult life from not just agoraphobia – but claustrophobia too.

As well as these fears, which could leave her hobbled on the doorstep for hours, havering over whether she should stay or go, she had one of flying as well. She was also visited by bizarre anxieties while holding a steering wheel. She once told me that the key safety measure to take when driving in the city was to look at the tyres of the parked cars on either side of the road. 'You can't see the bodies of children about to cross – but you can see their feet.'

I have spent the past twenty years looking for these children's feet, and although I've yet to see any I feel certain that one day my mother's advice will pay off and I'll be able to slam on the brakes in time to prevent myself macerating some headstrong juvenile. As I bucket over the speed bumps – an innovation my mother didn't live to see – I often feel her presence. She made even the most prosaic car journey into something uncertain and exciting by reacting to any untoward

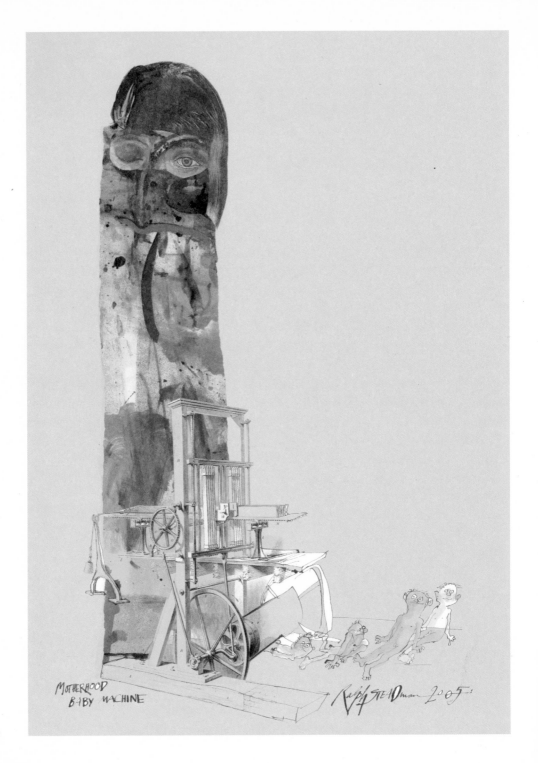

MOTHERHOOD
BABY MACHINE

stimuli – a pigeon's flight, a bus's whoosh – with a sharp intake of breath and an arm thrown across her passenger's torso.

But don't imagine that she was a nervous driver, on the contrary she was both fast and decisive. When I was a child she was contemptuous of the huts-on-wheels which passed for British cars. Rattling along in whichever duff Bedford or Austin we were condemned to that year, she'd regale me with tales of the six-cylinder Buick she'd driven in the States. A mighty beast of an auto, which could take the steepest hill at 65 mph in third. It wasn't until the last few years of her life that the car flesh on offer here came up to her standards, so she raced towards death with her foot jammed on the accelerator of a Ford XR3i.

After she was burnt at Golders Green Crematorium I took possession of both the car and Mother's ashes, which came in a bronze plastic container shaped like an enormous Nescafé jar. It was the final crisis of exile: what was to be done with them? Should Mother be scattered in her native or her adoptive country? As the daughter of a peripatetic man, whose own father had emigrated from Odessa to the USA, was there perhaps an argument for Mother, in death, completing the circular tour? I considered scattering her remains in the Black Sea.

Unable to muster a quorum of ash-scatterers – my siblings were far-flung – I found myself lumbered with Mother for some years. To begin with I kept her jar in the car, which doubtless explains that spectral arm and ghostly sharp intake of breath. I felt like the character played by Warren Oates in *Bring Me the Head of Alfredo Garcia*, and would often catch myself discoursing with Mother in a slightly crazed fashion. In time, it occurred to me that my inability to – in the requisite psycho-jargon – 'let go' of dead Mother might be because of her live phobias. The prospect of being interred had, presumably, terrified her quite as much as being cast to the winds, which was why she had been unable to express a preference.

I put her in the basement for a couple more years. Then, when the house was being sold, the idea of moving her as well – as if she were some middle-class urn burial – became too grotesque. My brothers and I eventually dusted Hampstead Heath with her grey powder and bony chunks. Her mulching spot is marked by a memorial slab commemorating her and a number of other Jewish people, most of whom probably also died of cancer. Such is the queer industry of souls.

# The Eden Reject

January 2043

Another New Year – another massive challenge. Power is, as ever, the problem. Since we first turned the former Mediterranean biome into a peat bog, we have had enough fuel to keep our own, larger biome at a habitable temperature: but now it looks as if the bog is ceasing to be self-sustaining. I idly raised the prospect at this morning's powwow of making a foray into the outside world: there must still be some abandoned vehicles on the old A30 which have intact petrol tanks.

However, I am now so old that the young of the community will not listen to me. They cannot remember the first years we spent here at the Project, or how – before the conditions outside utterly deteriorated – Martin Bulmer and I succeeded in siphoning many litres of petrol from the cars and buses which had brought us here. Without that fuel we never would've survived. The young Edenites care nothing for this – to them Bulmer and I are living fossils. I try to tell them that before the Gulf Stream switched off, and Britain was plunged into a new Holocene, the realm outside the Project was like the interior of the big biome: grassy hillsides studded with deciduous trees, neat fields of wheat, vegetable plots and orchards.

This they frankly disbelieve. They claim that the Project was created by a Supreme Ecologist and that the evidence of his wisdom is all around in the form of inspirational signs. Bulmer and I have tried to explain to them that these hokey quotes from Lao Tzu, Gandhi and Xenophon were placed in the biomes by very human designers, and that they should be taken as divine tablets is just one of the furious ironies of this paradoxical new era. Almost as furious as the fate of the Project itself, which was originally built as an exhibition of the earth's biodiversity, and has ended up as the final redoubt of human life in Britain – perhaps even the world.

Strange how extreme old age bestows such clarity of recollection. I can see myself

getting out of the family car in the Plum 1 parking zone as if it were yesterday. We walked down to the ticket booth marvelling at the way this old Cornish quarry had been transformed: its steep sides sculpted into artificial terraces, and at the bottom sat the two massive geodesic biomes, looking like alien spacecraft. At the time I thought the whole Eden Project faintly absurd. The Wee Man – a scarecrow constructed from the average amount of electrical equipment a Briton uses in his or her lifetime – set the tone. This was conservation dumbed down for the masses; a feel-better infotainment experience for those of us who had generated tons of hydrocarbons driving to see the thing. Just as the Great Exhibition had typified Britain's self-satisfied plundering of its imperium, so the Eden Project – under the guise of charity – was another exercise in rapacious acquisition.

We spent the morning strolling through the biomes. First the Mediterranean, which featured a campanile with a pantile roof, a *trompe-l'oeil* Harley Davidson, an adobe wall strewn with ponchos – chunks of scenery intended to offset the relevant flora. Then the massive tropical biome, in which a Malaysian stilt house and an Indian lorry were marooned within the towering and plangently artificial forest canopy. We lunched at Pasty Pod, watching another implant: a troupe of Rajasthani puppeteers. Looking out through the thick, hexagonal, polyurethane panels of the biome I could see the wintry landscape of Cornwall. Was it me, or did it look oddly parched and irradiated?

It wasn't me. A wall of ice spiracles swept down from the rim of the old quarry, lacerating the faces of anyone in the open. Families of eco-trippers ran for cover, their Gore-Tex jackets flayed from their torsos, their thermo-insulated fleeces no protection at all against this catastrophic spasm of climate change. Inside the biome the Rajasthani puppeteers were swept aside as panicking AA members foolishly made a sprint for their cars, which were already stranded in two-metre-deep drifts.

The first hectic months after the cataclysm were harsh. The thousand-odd visitors who were trapped inside the Eden Project were reduced to a couple of score by vicious fighting. It was amazing to see what savage ideological differences gripped these former denizens of bland Middle England once the civilising gloves were off. Eventually, Martin Bulmer – a bloody-minded estate agent from Cheadle – and I emerged as the undisputed leaders of the survivors. We instituted the draconian measures necessary to turn the former tourist attraction into a lifesaving ark.

Edmund Wilson, the respected founder of evolutionary biology, predicted that the next era would be dubbed 'the Eocene'. He thought humanity would be left alone upon a denuded earth. How ironic that instead a fragment of us should find ourselves alone in these linked biomes; ruled by a former estate agent.

# Flu Away!

Cases appear in clusters, way out in the boondocks of Zhengzou, where a man poling a sampan looks like a single, calligraphic stroke on the watery silk of the river. Until, that is, his lungs fill with fluid, and he begins to cough his lifeblood out. Nothing very Confucian about that; nothing pretty either about the small market towns where every imaginable animal – and some quite mythical beasts – is chopped up then hung up to be sold. The griffin with the chicken, the roc with the rat.

Cases appear in clusters, and the virus – which is a very small animal, although a hardy traveller – boards one avian cruise ship after another. The virus unpacks in its cabin, lays out its things, then goes in search of some entertainment – deck quoits or suchlike – only to discover that this vessel pitches and yaws and heaves quite as much as the last. The virus doesn't realise it has caused this, any more than the tourist appreciates he has destroyed a barrier reef or a rainforest. The virus jumps bird and boards another.

Cases appear in clusters – wherever humans and poultry snuggle up against one another in a tussle of grease, feathers and eggs. This interspecific kinkiness, this domestic violence – it's the very stuff of progress. If it weren't for all those many millennia of chicken lickin', the peoples of Eurasia wouldn't have been able to go forth and let the animal viruses – to which we had gained some immunity – wipe out the rest of the world's miserable indigenes.

Cases appear in clusters, and those clusters move steadily west. West across Vietnam, west across India and Pakistan, west through the Middle East, where people have more to worry about than a high fever. Westering, westering, until with a swish and flutter, a cough and a splutter, the cluster falls on Anatolia or Romania, splattering against the fabled cordon sanitaire. This diffusion, of course, prefigures the spread that is to come. For just as once virus rode upon flea, and

YOU COULD BE A CARRIER— DON'T COUNT YOUR CHICKENS!!

flea rode upon rat, and rat rode upon ship; so, when this little feller has got its act together, it'll have no need of cumbersome geese, unwieldy swans or clockwork barnyard fowl. Instead it'll relax in a fold-down extendable seat-bed, a cosy corpuscular cabin, inside a human that's inside a fold-down extendable seat-bed, inside a 747. Woosh! HN15 you are cleared for landing.

There have been outliers, precocious clusters in corrugated iron barns where the chicken holocaust is in full, daily swing. It's altogether mind-boggling that Belgian poultry farmers, striding in their rubber waders through agitated waves of starveling poultry, nonetheless managed to spot the foul-with-flu. But they did – and the predictable mass selection ensued: smoky barbecues under the Flemish moon, mmm! No one feels like chicken tonight.

Meanwhile in Hampstead and Harrogate and Harlech, eminent virologists make their own preparations. White goods are lined up to form chancels of health. The children are instructed on how to wash out their noses. Tamiflu is bought on the internet, in a job lot with this month's orders of Viagra and Prozac. Plans are made to endure a lengthy quarantine: they intend to remain housebound for months if necessary, trying out River Café recipes for guinea fowl with fennel, while outside in the streets hoi polloi hawk and spit.

From O.K. Chicken to Perfect Chicken, from Bootiful Chicken to Luvverly Chicken, from Royal Chicken to Chicken Imperium, from Chicken Universe to one forlorn joint in the filthy crotch of an abandoned shopping centre which is, quite simply, dubbed 'Chicken'. A farmer friend of mine once told me that the best thing to do if you wanted to get your chicken to taste really 'chickeny', was to feed your chicken . . . chicken. And so it is with the bird-flu-afflicted humans, for, in a hideous spasm of auto-cannibalism, they have decided to feed each to the other in pursuit of that most rare and piquant of delicacies – a truly 'humany' human.

I've always had an awkward relationship with birds – especially old human ones; I hate their alien stare, their hollow bones, their greasy feathers, their hard, pointed lips. I once wrote a vignette called 'The Enormous Chicken' in which a man's nemesis appears to him in just this form: a six-foot-high barnyard fowl that canters into his flat and pecks him to death on the Axminster. I have little faith in the Chief Medical Officer in the bunker of the Mass Disaster Room, moving his stocks of vaccine about on a map of the British Isles. We're better off gobbling down the parson's nose, then drying out the wishbone, hooking our little fingers about it and pulling. But don't tell anyone what you wished for.

The world may be big, but when there are upwards of six billion takeaway carriers an animal as small as a flu virus can bring it right down to size.

# The Green Zone

Consider the Green Zone – after all, somebody has to, so it might as well be you. Yes, you know about it – *tout le monde* does. It's the former mosh pit of the vile Ba'athist regime with which Saddam Hussein bludgeoned the Iraqi people for thirty-odd – very odd – years. And yes, it features a luxury canton for his henchmen, a leafy 'burb complete with splashing fountains, ornamental ponds and dinky bridges. There is also the string of grotesquely kitsch palaces, built on the banks of the Tigris for the dictator and his psychopathic sons. Uday had one for his lions, and one dedicated to the institutionalised rape that, for him, served as sexual congress.

Then there are the grand government buildings: the National Assembly, the Council of Ministers and the former Ba'ath party headquarters. Theirs is a decorticated modernism: the husk of administration, lying on the parched ground, ready to be infested by another maggot of Iraqi statehood – the Coalition Provisional Authority, the Interim Government and now, finally, the deeply democratic and fairly elected Government of the Iraqi people, by the Iraqi people, that just happens to contain Al-Qaeda sympathisers who are happy to allow their henchmen to smuggle bombs into their parliament building.

I digress. Perhaps the most titanic grotesquerie in the Green Zone are the two gigantic arms that hold crossed swords aloft over the parade ground where Saddam used to review the Republican Guard from an air-conditioned stand. I don't know whether these are still standing (and can one say of an arm that it ever stands at all?), but they were famously modelled on Saddam's own arms, right down to the hairs. No ancient Babylonian god-king could have been quite as gross as this, even when – as they were wont to do – they were reducing your house to a dungheap.

Perhaps the most unexpected thing about the ten square kilometres of the Green Zone, is quite how much empty space there is in it. By all accounts it's a citadel

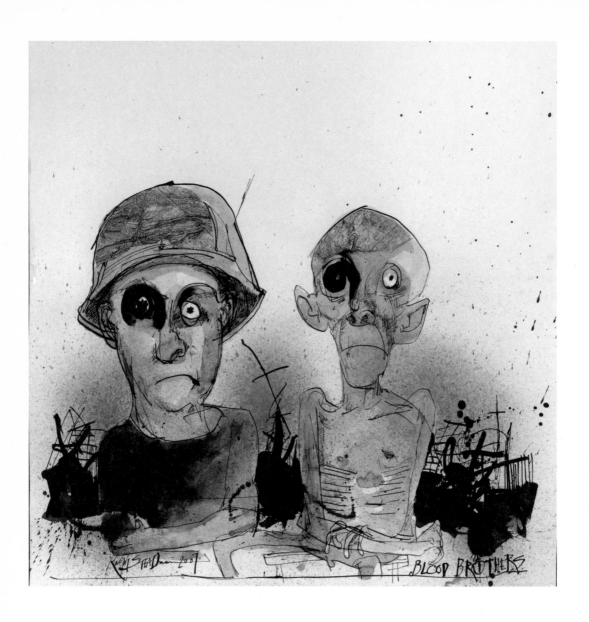

of dusty squares and wide boulevards where sandy zephyrs curl about the slow-moving, imported Jeep Grand Cherokees. Oh yes, I was almost forgetting, those SUVs are driven by the occupiers themselves. The officials, answerable to the Pentagon and the State Department, who, together with the private contractors sucking them off, number around 5,000.

They live in sandbagged modified shipping containers – designated 'housing modules' – and venture out to eat imported American food in feeding halls. There is a gym, they have satellite TV, and – you definitely knew this already – telephones with US area codes; so that they have to make overseas calls to the city without the concentric rings of blast walls, the razor wire, and the locked and loaded guards.

Much is made, and rightly so, of the Green Zone as a microcosm of the failure of US intervention in Iraq; of how the stepping into the shoes of the deposed Saddam combined with an inability to secure the Red Zone (you know what that is), to ensure that the Green Zone became more and more of a world apart, as psychically divorced from the violent hinterland it's trying to govern as Hawaii is physically separated from mainland America.

This is true – but obvious; more significant, in my view, are the 5,000 Iraqis who, under cover of the invasion, took vacant possession of the less grandiose villas of the fleeing Ba'athist apparatchiks. There's a nice symmetry in there being the same amount of these 'squatters' (they're only parenthetically so) as there are occupiers, for it makes of the Green Zone not a microcosm of an idea – 'failure', 'success', 'security' – but a kind of emergent society in its own right. This, one feels, is the shape of territories to come.

In the last few weeks US forces have completed their construction of a concrete wall around the Baghdad district of Adhamiya. The aim of the ten-foot-high concrete barrier is to keep the Sunni 'militants' in, but the prevailing Iraqi view is that it creates a pressure cooker waiting to explode. As it is for Baghdad and Palestine so it may be for the US. The rising sea of overheated humanity laps against our moneyed shores – they're gatecrashing our barbecue and they weren't even invited! Keep 'em out. Build the flood barrier.

Perhaps the last thing to be said about the Green Zone is to hearken back to its pre-2003 name, 'the Emerald City'. I'm not sure if *The Wizard of Oz* was ever prominent among the *samizdat* literature that was – and is – sold on the back streets of Baghdad, but one thing's for certain: this was spot-on. For just as Saddam turned out to be a little old man, operating his huge arms by wires, so the West's attempts to impose its own image on an unwilling world are beginning to look like nothing but make-believe.

# The Inertia
# of Middle Age

I yearn for a fixed wheel bicycle – it is the very epitome of my midlife crisis. For those of you not familiar with such a contrivance, let me elucidate. With most bicycles you can free-wheel with your feet on the pedals, but with a fixed wheel you have to pedal all the time. The chain is directly connected to the sprocket, so in order to brake you pedal slower – or even backwards. You see quite a number of people riding fixed wheel bicycles in London, and they all have certain things in common: they are young, fit, and obviously have no preoccupation with mortality whatsoever. They believe they are going to pedal for ever.

Cycling through heavy traffic with no means of arresting your onward rush save your own legs, must – I theorise – introduce a peculiarly Zen cast of mind. The fixed wheel cyclist has to be constantly attuned to the myriad, random possibilities of the urban thoroughfare, while at the same time feeling his translation through space as a constant muscular phenomenon. This 1:1 ratio means that fixed wheel cycling is the closest you can get to being a robot while still being sentient. The bicycle itself is stripped down to its most basic elements – wheel, frame, chain – while the rider's mind is, perforce, empty of all save the phenomenon of its own inertia.

My conversations with ex-fixed wheel cyclists have tended to confirm my suppositions. They give it up – they say – because it's impossible to pay any attention to their surroundings while straddling such a nerve-racking vehicle. I can't verify this by talking to people who are still doing it, because they're virtually incapable of communication at all, but lost in a trance in which they apprehend the traffic flows outside of space and time. Perhaps they can actually 'see' the truck before it lurches out of the side street, or the arc of the cab before it performs an extempore three-point turn? What else could explain their willingness to pit Lycra against steel?

It all puts me in mind of a short story I once wrote (so much does nowadays,

another function of the midway point), called 'Waiting', in which a secret cabal of London motorcycle couriers are in thrall to a seer called Carlos. Carlos *can* do what I think the fixed wheel cyclists ought to be capable of – and much more. Simply by observing the traffic flow on one road, for a few minutes, he can extrapolate an entire mental picture of the road system of London, complete with all its jams, queues and chance contretemps. The followers of Carlos become privy to this arcane method, and so never have to wait for anything.

It's the curse of the speculative writer to see his fictional creations cancelled out by the prosaic march of time. The global positioning satellite systems – which now sucker on to even the most battered and lowly of cars – are the plastic form the mystic cabal has taken. Why it is, that the authorities haven't proscribed devices which encourage drivers to stare fixedly at a tiny screen featuring a schematic representation of where they are, rather than *looking* at the real world, is beyond me. Or rather, I understand the commercial realities only too well: just as with the mobile phone, until there is total market saturation, there will be no check placed on the use of GPS in cars.

By then, far from having created a population of lean ascetics, whose total orientation confirms their state of oneness with the world, we will have spawned an entire generation of obese fuck-wits, who won't have the slightest idea where they are, once de-coupled from their navigation systems, and levered from their warm leatherette. Where they are – or even, what they should do. At least the old-fashioned road map placed the onus of arrival on our own cognitive abilities; now we are beginning to abrogate all responsibility. Paradoxically, the long and tortuous drive away from mass transit systems and towards the 'freedom' of the private car, turns out to have been a circular tour. With GPS and the onboard computers there will, presumably, soon be to 'do' the driving, everyone on the road will be in possession of what is effectively their own rail system. A mono-carriage train, running one scheduled journey, on a track lain for that journey alone.

We are tugboats gone crazy, with no idea even if we are in a safe harbour, or churning up the soil! We are dragging the rusting hulks of the past into the shiny future! We are speedboats that have quit the water to describe loop-the-loops in a dark sky near to the end of history! The seagulls – those fixed wheel cyclists of the sky – are ripped away from their thermals by our crazy jigging, and stare at us, at once terrified and contemptuous.

# The Yurt

It all begins at the Ron Mueck exhibition, which has been mounted in the National Gallery of Scotland, on Princes Street in Edinburgh. The Australian sculptor laboriously fashions intensely lifelike figures out of pliable synthetics. Some say these manikins are mere kitsch – not art at all. But I love them. All the more so because they're defiantly out of scale. The first Mueck I recall seeing was his 'Dead Dad' at the infamous 1997 Royal Academy 'Sensation' exhibition. There was Mueck's own deceased father, lain out on a plinth on the gallery floor, exact in every regard, right down to the limp snail of his curled penis, but only one-sixth life size.

In Brobdingnag, the Queen's giant ladies-in-waiting set Gulliver astride their nipples and jounced him up and down. So it is with Mueck's giant newborn babies and diminutive, gossiping old women: they invite you to touch them, yet simultaneously repel. They are so human, so present – and yet profoundly alien, totally absent. For slightly solipsistic types such as myself, they project feeling like a death ray: the brobdingnagian, naked man clutching the seat of his chair in terror; the even more Pantagruelian woman, recumbent and miserable beneath a duvet the size of a bungalow.

On this occasion the Muecks did their thing, and nothing in Edinburgh was the same size for the rest of my stay, while my emotions ran amok. This was no bad thing, because I usually find Festival time drags on me like a sea anchor: all those bum-fluffy, wannabe thespians ramming flyers for Shavian comedies into your hand, the motley crews of unfunny comedians, cack-handed jugglers and congested nose flute-players that wander the streets, reduce me to a quietly gibbering introversion. With so many people acting up, I feel like adopting a foetal position in a dark corner.

No chance of that in room 306 of the Bonham Hotel. Otherwise nondescript, the huge bay window looks out due north, over the Firth of Forth and to the

WILL'S EYE VIEW

Ralph STEADman 2006

uplands beyond. It is a humungous view: a full 180 degrees, a radius of perhaps forty miles. I sleep with the curtains open, so that the dawn drags me out into the open air, soaring over Leith, across to Fife, up to Perth, swooping down over Loch Tay. I am Harry-bloody-Potter and my bolster has become a dream broomstick.

Later, at the Book Festival, which is encamped in Charlotte Square, I encounter the Director next to the 'Authors' Yurt'. 'Why the yurt again?' I query. 'You always have a yurt; shouldn't other traditional peoples get a look-in? Why can't there be an authors' Hogan, or longhouse, or igloo?' She is quite unfazed: 'Strictly speaking it shouldn't be called a yurt at all, the correct name for it is a ger.' Grrr! Indeed. The BookFest is, after all, a transient culture, like that of the Mongols. The huddle of gers, tents and marquees are connected by boardwalks, along which progress the nomads – so-called 'authors' and their 'readers'.

After a fortnight or so the whole camp will be struck and moved on to Bath or Buxton or Cheltenham. The BookFesters seem to favour the rather more genteel British towns with their presence – although they don't lay waste to them. About the only equestrian feature of this Edinburgh encampment is the statue on a plinth in the centre of the square. A statue which, a few years ago, my then four-year-old son – displaying a sensibility that Gulliver would've relished – tried vainly to touch, crying out: 'Horsey, I can't reach it!'

That night, together with a trio of other writers, and a solo publisher, I ate at the Witchery, a themed restaurant at the top of the Royal Mile. I'm not quite sure what the theme is, unless it's something to do with the fact that scores of poor women were burnt here for 'witchcraft' during the medieval era. I shudder to think what the themed restaurants of the future will be like . . . Anyway, the Edinburgh Tattoo was in full swing as we stumbled up the cobbles of Castlehill, cannons boomed, cymbals clashed, the stands full of spectators soared up over the Castle walls. It was as if the entire Nuremberg Rally were banged up in a little cell.

We left the restaurant in time with the massed ranks of the Black Watch pipe band. Huge men, skirling for all they were worth. In between them marched proud Gurkhas, in their tight, black uniforms. 'Those are the ones to watch out for,' I told one of my companions, 'it's axiomatic that there's no man more angry than a Scot under five feet five. No one, that is, save for a Nepalese in a Scots regiment.' One of the Gurkhas must've heard me, for he bared his teeth: 'Grrr . . .' just like a Mueck on the move.

# Come Dancing

Here's a picture of Madeleine Valedon warming up for the first live broadcast of 'Allons La Dance!' from the now famous Radio France studio underneath the Pont Neuf. The year was 1948 and French manhood was in a pitiful state: those Frenchmen who hadn't been emasculated by occupation, were gelded by collaboration. A few brave fellows had taken to the *maquis*, only to discover that the thorns grievously scratched their testicles.

But that night the brilliant flash of Madeleine's petticoats awakened them all! Their dormant blood vessels began to stir to the hot rhythms of Les Jazzeurs, and when the outfit was joined by Django Reinhardt on guitar and Jean-Paul Sartre on flugelhorn, the joint really began to jump. That first broadcast was watched by a colossal audience of ninety-four, of whom thirty alone were in the Élysée Palace. De Gaulle himself is said to have arisen from his uncomfortable Louis Quinze armchair and essayed a few steps on the echoing marble floor. A nation was reborn – and all through the power of the dance!

I recall this because I was out dancing last weekend, and it occurred to me that just like any other form of physical activity, dance mediates place. The following morning a friend called me up: 'You were spotted last night,' he told me, as if I had committed some fearful indiscretion, 'dancing at Shoreditch Town Hall.' It was true, it was me, and worse still: I'd been dancing with my wife! How louche can you get? We rose from our Eton mess to join some of the other wedding guests, who were bobbing about on the wide expanse of parquet. On the stage itself was a DJ at the turntables, and a lot of little girls in lovely party dresses, gyrating with that complete fusion of abandonment and unselfconsciousness that only the pre-pubescent can really achieve.

As I minced hither and thither, I took in my surroundings: the high, panelled and gilded walls of the chamber; the enormous swags of curtain either side of the stage. It all spoke of solid, nineteenth-century municipal pride – and so I began to adjust my terpsichorean promenade accordingly. I strutted and preened as if my collar were trimmed with fur. I stuck my face to the floor, so as to give the impression that my neck was weighed down by a heavy chain of office. I shook my fist in the air as if I were ringing a bell and cried out 'Oyez! Oyez!' Any old fool can dance in time, but dancing in place takes real élan.

Ah! Dancing – it's wasted on the young. When you're a young man, in the full blush of burgeoning sexuality, dancing can be a bit of a torment. As I bopped to 'Killer Queen' in my asinine, bell-bottomed trousers, I could never quite rid myself of the suspicion that my every spasm and contortion was being filmed by secret cameras, and that soon this footage would be screened in the local Odeon, so that all my so-called friends could come along to laugh and point.

True, young women seem to dance quite happily together, but I don't believe them to be where they physically are when they do it. Rather, they are transported into a parallel bower, and here they frolic, like stateless naiads. The male dance is an agonised demonstration of putative prowess, a mapping out of desire: 'Come to my place,' the he-bee buzzes, 'I've got lots of alcoholic honey.' By contrast, the dancing queens are so many pretty blooms all in row. The more they move, the more they remain static, luring us insects into their flytraps.

But all of this is in time – not in place. Dancing in place is complex and initiatory. It speaks of society – not only sex. I remember being on the fringes of the Barkly Tablelands in Northern Australia, and watching the young lads of an Aboriginal mob practising for their initiation. Looked at one way, their dancing was unspectacular: a series of short skips, a brief hoedown in the dust accompanied by an ululation from the company, then they ran off again. Yet concentrated in their movements were all the red dirt expanses that spread out to the horizon; the crumbling ranges of ancient hills; the conical, raised waterholes of the white Australian ranchers. I'd never seen people dance so fervently in place before.

Or at least, not since I myself, wired to pinging point on amphetamine sulphate, juddered, gobbed and bashed into my comrades like a humanoid bowling ball. That was dancing in place, and the place was this piss-stinky basement club, or that trashed squat. Our spasms and isms were our celebration of place, our drunken cries our ululation, and for those frenzied hours we were quite as aboriginal as any teenagers, anywhere.

UP AND OFF IN PARIS

# Burning an Illusion

Margate at the fag end of September. We arrived in the late afternoon with the sun slanting in on the seafront. Next to the station stands the enormous, wrinkled digit of Arlington House, a Brutalist twenty-storey block of flats that seems to waggle a warning at all asylum seekers: 'Enter this land of promise, and you'll be banged up in here for ever.' Or worse, in the decaying terrace of the Nayland Rock refugee hostel. Once this was a luxury hotel, now it houses Roma on the run from central Europe; Congolese fleeing the meltdown of central Africa; Iraqis evading the maelstrom of the Middle East. Strange, that so many people escaping the dread gravity of these landmasses should find themselves clinging on to the very tip of the Isle of Thanet, which in turn is like a cold sore on the Kentish lip of old England.

In the sharp sunlight every zit and pore on every promenading face was brought into sharp focus. The fast food joints were doing a roaring trade in chip-shaped grease, the boy racers were roaring along the strip, the change-gobbling amusement parlours don't seem funny at all. Yet the sea was placid. So much so, that people walking along the dividers of the old seawater swimming pools seemed to be strolling atop the waves. And the beach was a beautifully clean sable swathe, dotted here and there with amiable gaggles of metropolitan art-lovers, exiled from their salubrious city.

We were members of the same tribe: there to witness the Margate Exodus, a day-long experimental film version of the biblical fable, which saw its director, Penny Woolcock, incorporate actors and townspeople into a free-flowing narrative. The whole festive event culminated in the burning of the Waste Man, a huge sculpture assembled out of discarded wooden furniture under the direction of Antony Gormley.

I have to say, the stated aims of the Exodus – to call attention both to the foreign exilics and the internal exile of Margate's disadvantaged – struck me as just a

JUNK FOOD MAN UNDER A MARGATE TURNER SUNSET

BUY 50
GET
15 FREE

Ralph STEADman 2006

little patronising when I heard about them. It hardly seemed likely that the furious – often quasi-fascistic – denizens of Thanet, were going to respond to the arthouse filmic conceit by throwing their arms around the inmates of Nayland Rock in a gesture of human solidarity. Nor could I envision the burning of a lot of old chairs becoming the fire from which the phoenix of Margate's civic beauty would be reborn. But that was before I saw Waste Man in all his fleshly, wooden glory, towering up above the defunct rollercoasters of Margate's Dreamland Funfair. His peculiar, 3-D collage of a body was reminiscent of a giant Arcimboldo, devised to remind us all, that all is vanity.

We liaised with the Waste Man's Frankenstein at the Harbour Café, and he and I went off for a swim in the placid sea. We struck out towards the lighthouse, and from out there on the gently heaving swell, Margate appeared as a fantastical, post-apocalyptic city. The two of us shared a scrap of towel, then Antony went off to arrange his detonators, while I gathered up the family and followed in his wake. The whole of Margate seemed to be gravitating towards Dreamland; crowds of all ages and ethnicities, pasty, tanned and tattooed. If anything united them it was a curious silence – there was no buzz of anticipation, only a surly quiescence. Would it break out into violence, I wondered, if the Waste Man failed to perform?

We got into the back-concrete-apron area of the burning, and marshalled the children on a wheelie bin. Waste Man stood a couple of hundred feet off. He was fully a hundred feet high, and dwarfed the experimental actors who were dangling off his belly on winches. I couldn't pay any mind to this performance; and nor, I think, could the vast crowd now assembled below. We only had eyes for Waste Man: we craved his fiery sacrifice. Dusk folded its moth wings about us. The moon came up in the north-west, a train clacked into the station. Waste Man stood, implacable, one arm raised in sturdy defiance.

Then, with a sudden 'crack', smoke began to pour from his belly and lick up his chest. He was on fire – and so were we. I have no paradigm for what it's like to watch an enormous wooden figure burn – save perhaps the film of *The Wicker Man*. But without fear of hyperbole, let me tell you, it was a beautiful sight. The silence of the crowd shifted from surly to awed, and we were all moved. Perhaps that was the mystery of the Margate Exodus? A voluntary exile, away from the gnawing ills of the early twenty-first century, and towards some deeper, darker, still hungrier place and time.

# From a Dope
# to a Burqa

It's a weekend in mid-November: the Chancellor of the Exchequer, and heir apparent to the British Premiership, Gordon 'Steady Hand' Brown, is in Basra, Iraq. The avatar of his credo, Tony 'Air Guitar' Blair, is on his way to Helmand Province, Afghanistan. Meanwhile, I'm in Amsterdam, in a 'coffee shop' near the Nieuwmarkt called the Green Seed Company. Not, you understand, that I've smoked dope for years now, it's just that the habit of watching people's habits dies hard, and I'm intrigued to see what's happened to the Netherlands' famed policy of tolerance in the decade-or-so since I was last here.

Tolerance is not quite the right word when it comes to the Dutch, because the truth is that they have a gritted-teeth conservatism about them. The narrow, high-gabled merchants' houses that line the elegant, old canals of the city centre are a reification of the national character: functional – with their protruding winches – and betraying their opulence not in ornamentation but the lack of it. Rich puritans, bummer, eh? And get this, even as a plume of fumes from some dead-head's joint full of Super Silver Haze snakes up my nostril, the outgoing immigration minister, Rita Verdonk, is campaigning hard for the forthcoming Dutch general election. Her pledge: to take out that troublesome black bag, the Muslim burqa.

You don't have to be stoned to wonder exactly to what extent Gordon Brown actually feels himself to be in Iraq, or for that matter, Blair in Helmand. Colleagues, who've covered these grubby wars on the ground, tell me that the notion that the British forces have won hearts and minds more than the Americans is utter balderdash. Unless on patrol, securely behind armour, and with a heavy machine gun trained on the civilian population, our boys are confined to their heavily fortified barracks. Here, behind blast walls and razor wire, they watch beamed-in soap operas, and have roast meals. The aircon hums – while without it's roasting.

Still, however misguided, at least the troops have a role; and even if their situation

SMOKING
BURGER
WOMAN.

Ralph STEADman

SOFT
DRINKS
MAN.
2006.

VIAGRA
MAN. DICKHEAD'

is somewhat unreal, the sheer length of the tours they have to serve means that sooner or later the reality of where they are will impinge. We hope not fatally. They're there because they're there. Not so Blair and Brown, the Tweedledum and Tweedledumber of British foreign policy. See them stride across the sandy, rubble-strewn bled! See their bright eyes, narrowing in the glare to statesmanlike slits. We have returned! their purposeful attitudes convey, as surely as if they were MacArthur, sucking on his outsize corncob, while humiliating Japanese warlords on the deck of his aircraft carrier.

Brown looks even more rugger-bugger than usual in his Kevlar embonpoint. What can he be saying, as he sits himself down for the school-style photo-op, surrounded by young men who couldn't give a toss about him, or his long-awaited satrapy. Perhaps: 'D'you know where the hell we are, lads?' Neither the flak jacket nor the Hercules flight will have altogether orientated him, for given what a political coward he is – suckled for a decade now on the wormwood-smeared teat of self-advancement – he probably wears bullet-proof pyjamas. What a burqa.

And what berks the English in Amsterdam are. Leaving the Green Seed coffee shop I proceed up the Gelderse Kade. The merchandise in these elegant houses is women. Poor Dutch girls, trafficked East Europeans, Moluccan immigrants – all togged out in their so-sexy undies. Up for the grabs of beery boys from Brum, the brothers of the ones in Basra. Look at those hordes of stoned, drunken English! How they wheel and butt, like musk oxen on the arctic tundra, as they weather their storms of toxicity. Around them circle lean packs of Surinamese drug dealers; 'Coke?' they importune, 'Coke?', again and again.

It isn't easy to be cynical – it's demanding work that requires a man fit for purpose. Here are the English: ensconced in their drug base, protected by blast walls of hash and lines of razor-wire cocaine, while all round them is nothing save the featureless desert of Dutch rectitude. Do they, I wonder, actually know where they are? They've flown into Schiphol, taken the train to Centraal Station, and staggered into their picturesque saturnalia. Their only mission is to enjoy themselves, and they're here because of a fiscal compromise that Gordon Brown might be proud of: the pimps and dealers do good business, but they pay their taxes just like anyone else.

As I regain the yellow-light district and enter the marbled, corporate hall of my hotel, the Barbizon, I muse on Rita Verdonk. Will she hang on to power with her VDU Liberal Party? Will she rip the burqas from the twenty-odd Dutch Muslims who are estimated to wear them? And how is it that a nation which can withstand such brazen, English rubbish, has so little tolerance for bin-bag couture?

# My Second Life

I wonder, can you read this? By which I mean to say: am I being heard? Because that's what we all really care about, isn't it, being heard, our words having value through their being understood by another? A few months ago, I probably would've said 'another human being'; however, I'm not so sure whether I know what that means any more, or indeed, if I'm one myself.

Let me explain. We all know that 2006 has been *the* year for user-generated web content: all those snapshots of gurning teenagers, all those belligerent bloggers' opinions. The internet is a worldwide corkboard, on to which are tacked the reminder notes of millions. How can the common hack stand his ground in such a deluge of self-publishing? I began to feel exiguous: a ghost in the machine of my own literary production. Worse than that, I also started to feel insubstantial in the domestic sphere: my children looked through me, my wife – on one, chilling occasion – reached for the salt and was surprised to find my torso in the way.

Depressed, I took to spending more and more time shut up in my room, surfing the web. I bought more books than anyone could read – even in a lifetime. I sold my toenail clippings on eBay. I hung out in chat rooms. None of it worked, I was, if anything, more insignificant than ever. Then I discovered Second Life, a virtual world. Second Life – for those of you who are pig-ignorant Neanderthals – is an online, three-dimensional society, created by its own residents. To play, you log on and create your own 'avatar', an idealised version of yourself, who can act out your fantasies in this shiny, pixelated realm.

Second Life's creator, Philip Linden, has said that he wanted to create a world 'better than reality, but without political or religious issues'. I say, why the qualifier, Phil? Because a world without political and religious issues is, ipso facto, far better than a miserable, hate-fuelled dirt ball, with spit-streaked pavements and rubbish-strewn hospital wards. And while we're at it, why not a world without real sexual

NEW YORK CITIZEN-2. *Ralph STEADman*

issues either? For, certainly, Second Life conforms to this ideal. I mean, you could try and get it on with your fellow avatars; but why bother, when the experience offers all the sensory delights of caressing a microwave oven with an oven glove.

I took to Second Life like a duck to clay shooting. I bought a bundle of 'Linden dollars' (the local currency), leased a condo, and set about establishing my avatar (Dirk Bignib), as . . . a writer. I discovered, joyously, that shorn of the complicating factors – such as sex, religion and politics – which, in the 'real' world, rendered my fiction off-putting to the majority of book-buyers, I was able to churn out highly successful novels. Of course, Dirk Bignib is altogether without the feeble, left-wing scruples that made earning a lot of money from trash seem vulgar to 'Will Self'; and Second Life, being a defiantly capitalistic sort of place, gave me plenty of opportunities to spend my money on covetable major brands such as Sony and Nike.

Within six months of joining Second Life, I was earning more money from my writing there than I was on earth. Better still, I'd given up smoking. (By this, I mean Dirk Bignib didn't smoke, 'Will Self' was still puffing away like a trooper, and becoming increasingly emaciated, since he couldn't leave his keyboard to eat, or wash, or even shit.) Staggering downstairs from another eighty-seven-hour session in Second Life, I encountered my wife (at least, I think it was her, she seemed so exiguous and unreal); she looked at the skinny, hairy travesty of my 'body', and whispered: 'I do not know you'.

I took this as a green flag to carry on. By last month, I was spending almost my entire life in Second Life, only coming back to the dull, old first world to grab the occasional bowl of muesli. Then, horror of horrors, tragedy struck. One morning, leaving my beautifully appointed condo, and about to step into my bright-red BMW, I, Dirk Bignib, chanced to look up at the sky, and saw hanging there a terrifying apparition, with a long beard and wreathed in cloudy vapours. Religion had entered Second Life! I sank to my knees, only to realise that far from being a sky god, this was none other than my discarded 'human' visage, looking into my virtual world.

Still screaming, I drove to the nearest cybercafé, slung the clerk a couple of Lindens and logged on to my server. I've no idea whether it's possible to send an email from a virtual world to a real one, but it has to be worth a try. You see, I'm trapped in here, a pathetic victim of my own search for significance. But then you understand that, don't you . . . ? Don't you . . . ? Don't . . .

# The Sordid Act
# of Union

Now that it looks likely that the Act of Union will be dissolved, and after 300 years, fair Albion will be divorced by her long-abused partner, dour, post-traumatic-disordered Caledonia, it's time we started looking around for new countries we'd like our own nations to get married to.

I asked the psychologist Oliver James, an old friend of mine, and the author of *Britain on the Couch*, what he thought the likely impact of the divorce will be on our respective national psyches. His remarks – which I reproduce below – were unequivocal:

'Contrary to her expectations, unhappy Caledonia will not, necessarily, find herself liberated by ending this relationship. Many countries leave abusive unions, only to find that they can't sustain intimacy with a new partner – even if only for the purposes of trade. They tend to imagine themselves as living the life of a gay divorcee, strutting about on the international stage, conducting exciting diplomatic affairs with other single countries. The reality is very different.'

'Meaning?'

'Well, think of Slovakia and the Czech Republic; together they made a great team, but now they're just the political equivalent of sad old single men, sitting in their string vests, brewing up tea in some *mittel*-European bedsit.'

'That's harsh.'

'I am harsh.'

'But hang on a minute, you said "gay" divorcee, you don't mean to say –?'

'That Scotland is, in modern parlance, homosexual? Yes, that's exactly what I meant to say. Indeed, part of Scotland's great tragedy is that it has this overbearing, masculine image of itself as a country, while in reality it's very much been the femme to butch England.'

'And England?'

FOREIGN PARTS

Ralph STEADman 2007

'Ah, perfidious Albion, a flirty-dirty kind of a country if ever there was one. You only have to consider the way that England lured France on.'

'But presumably, you're referring to the revelation that in September 1956 the Anglophile French Premiere, Guy Mollet, proposed to the then British Prime Minister, Anthony Eden, that the two countries should, um, merge – if that doesn't sound too kinky?'

'That's right.'

'On that basis, I fail to see how you can accuse England of "luring" France on.'

'You obviously haven't looked at a map recently. Consider this: Britain is often depicted as anthropoid landmass, with Cornwall as its leg, East Anglia as its rump, and so on. It follows that ever since the collapse of the land bridge linking us to the continent, England has been, er, exposing herself to bashful France. Poor France, compelled for aeons to stare at the enlarged pudendum of the Isle of Wight!'

'You're being absurd! If you follow this mad, cartographic logic, then Scotland is Britain's head, and Wales its arms and embonpoint. It follows that there could be no seduction of France without these other nations' compliance.'

'I don't know about that, some countries find headless nations enormously attractive, surely that's why we class colonialism as a perversion. Anyway, that's neither here nor there, although I am glad you brought up the issue of Wales – and Ireland for that matter.'

'I didn't mention Ireland.'

'No matter, I did. The best definition of Ireland is, in fact, a definition of Russia: "Imagine the Irish with an empire".'

'Do you think that's funny?'

'It's not *not* funny. Look, the point is this: once Scotland and England are divorced, Wales and Ireland will be in a very tricky situation, their loyalties divided, forced to spend one weekend with one divorced parent, the next at the other's. These sorts of things can deeply traumatise a small nation.'

'You don't mean to suggest that Wales and Ireland are in some sense *children* of Scotland and England? Surely, this conception of the British Isles is deeply offensive to all concerned?'

'I'm glad you mentioned conception, because the Isle of Man is a still-viable, embryonic nation, created by Scotland and England without the authority of the United Nations Fertilisation Authority, and that proves that the Act of Union was always more in the nature of a civil partnership, than a marriage in the biblical sense.'

'You're in cloud cuckoo land –'

'An interesting nation, but beside the point.'

'Which is?'

'Look, I'm going out on an isthmus here, but I'm not absolutely certain that Scotland ever really was gay.'

'Aha! Decided you'd like to live out your days in peace, did you?'

'Nor do I wish to voice that old canard about predatory homosexual countries, but you have to concede that England did spend an awful lot of time in the Roman, ah, empire. Freud viewed international relations as only really successful when what he termed "full genitality" was achieved. By which he meant the deep penetration of one nation by another's, um, territory.'

'What're you driving at here?'

'That it may be time for Scotland to try a union with a more masculine country.'

'Such as?'

'Germany springs to mind.'

# Desktop Santiago

The Santiago Metro could make any other mass urban transit system feel like a rad-dled old whore. I'm staying in a flashy hotel in the upmarket El Golf district, and from the tenth floor this teeming Latin American capital appears cluttered with the banal forms of mirror-shiny buildings. They transform the city into a desktop covered with modular trays: are there office workers in that one, or paper clips?

But the Metro, now there's a thing. I've never come across a subway station with its own preserved fruit shop *and* lending library. There are also oil paintings on the platforms, and how clean is that? They're big, well-lit canvases of seaside views and rural farms; perhaps a little neo-realist for my taste – but you can't have every-thing. Hell, in Santiago, if you so desire, you can ride smoothly into the centre of town, while reading a Spanish translation of Ken Follett, and stuffing yourself with peaches in syrup. Moscow, eat your dark heart out.

Downtown the Torre Entel looms over all. It's homey to be in a country where a monopolistic telecommunications company has planted a 200-metre-high con-crete caber in the ground, then stuck a steely yoghurt pot on top. Perhaps the Torre explains why Chileans are called 'the English of Latin America'? It could be this, or it could be the riot control trucks, complete with rotating water cannons, that patrol the streets around the old presidential palace in the Plaza de Armas. Mmm, so *à la recherche de* Falls Road.

They have a cosy yet threatening look, these battered, brown, bullet-dimpled trucks. Wire mesh has been artfully shaped over their windscreens and wing mir-rors; they circle the square under the blank, granite façades of 1930s office blocks that are also pockmarked by gunfire, on one of which hangs a banner showing a handshake, and the one-word slogan: *Mediacion*.

Funny old Chile, eh? the Latin American country that works. The Chileans are sober, industrious, then in 1973 they went bonkers in the nut, and the air force

151

FOR VICTOR JARA

HEIGHT IS EVERYTHING

SALVADOR
ALLENDE
GOSSENS

ART

strafed and bombed the presidential palace, while, inside, the incumbent, Salvador Allende, topped himself. Even now, Santiago feels like a decapitated capital, with the Head of State floating in a jar of preserved fruit.

During the Pinochet years, the Plaza de Armas was tunnelled under to create a paranoid network of dictatorial bunkers, but in recent years there's been a democratic dividend, and instead of the nation's history being connived at underground, some of the bunkers have been turned into the Museum of National History.

The presidential palace was rebuilt – but only as a theme park version of itself. Now, through its off-white-walled courtyards, past the plashing fountains, their epaulettes tickled by palm fronds, come marching astonishing squads of girl-soldiers in Ruritanian uniforms: shiny-peaked caps, figure-hugging off-white tunics, olive-green breeches with satin stripes down the side, blancoed bandoliers, patent-leather knee boots with spurs. They're as yummy as chocolate soldiers, while their male counterparts in the Presidential Guard seem freakishly elongated.

Allende himself is commemorated by a sculpture in front of the palace, which is of such overpowering ugliness, it's difficult not to conclude that the Chileans revile him with a passion. The once mild and professorial socialist leader is depicted with a horse-brush moustache and spectacles as thick-rimmed as welder's goggles. He strides forward on his plinth, the sharp lines of his double-breasted suit blurred by a strange, thick membrane, which I stared at for some minutes, before realising that it was meant to be the Chilean flag.

Ah, Santiago! With your quaint old stationers, with your little carts selling *motte con huesille*, a traditional soft drink compounded from boiled corn and peach juice, while, in the next precinct, global Goths munch flame-grilled Whoppers to the 'pop-pop-pop' of automated pedestrian crossings.

At the Church of San Francisco there's a terrifying shrine. In a gold-framed, glass cabinet, sits Our Saviour, chopped off at the waist, his hair human, his stigmata spray-painted, and bracketed by mad flower arrangements. Poor Jesus, he looks like a mechanical model at the end of the pier of faith. Put a penny in his box and he'll start to lick his wounds.

Back at the hotel it's time for me to feel acute self-pity. The turn-down service have come, and besides ensuring that there are thirty-four large white pillows on the bed, on top of a white chocolate, they've re-enacted a scene from The Shining in the bathroom: five inches of bloody, perfumed bathwater have been drawn, a candle lit on the tile surround, and beside this has been placed a glass of red wine. Instead of feeling pampered I'm freaked out and embattled, the fighter-bombers are strafing the desk top, and it's time for me to fall on my paper clip.

# Chile con Carne

We're eating at Doña Tina, a restaurant in the 'burbs to the east of Santiago that has been recommended to us as distinctively Chilean. We were driven out here by one of the plush hotel cars, and swishing over overpasses, and swooping through underpasses, we might have been anywhere in the developed world. Still, I've read my stats; I know that although the average income here is around $12,000 per annum, 40 per cent of the population still remain below the UN poverty line. Even so, if Chile is the England of South America, Santiago is doing a remarkably good job of looking like its Basingstoke.

And if Santiago is Basingstoke, then Doña Tina is its Angus Steakhouse. Perhaps this is a distinctively Chilean eating experience, these acres of empty, red-and-white check, plastic tablecloths, the warm breeze soughing in the rustic, thatched trellises that overarch them. I try to tell myself this, as a bullish waiter charges out from the faux-Bavarian-bodega of the restaurant's interior, but I'm not convinced: it's Saturday night, and we're the only customers.

It gets more Basingstoke by the second, because the menu features photographs of the available dishes. Despite this, we still manage to balls-up the ordering – or possibly not. We get a pig product platter to start: slices of thick, fatty ham; parings of dark, smoked ham; chunks of pork pâté; circlets of compressed pig's head – complete with sections of brain, skull and sweetmeats.

Next up is an enormous fist of a fillet steak, with two orangey knuckles of fried egg. It's garnished with a Jenga tower of chips, and comes with a dish of pulped corn wrapped in a cornhusk. This food isn't heavy – it's ballast. This is food to take on board before you cast off from Chile's elongated coastline and head out into the turbulent swell of the Pacific.

An hour later the driver picks us spheroids up and rolls us back into town. Swishing along the Basingstoke bypass he brakes by the entrance to a dubious establishment with two flaming torches by its entrance.

'You gentlemen want to go to the nightclub?' he calls over his shoulder. I can see two burly bouncers, and the name of the club in neon letters: 'WOMN'. The absence of the crucial vowel suggests an ambience beyond the sordid. I picture leering satyrs, with botched chimeras from the island of Dr Moreau gyrating inches above their big top laps.

'Er, no,' my companion Marc says, 'I think we'll pass on that one.' Indeed, even if our porky flesh were remotely willing, it's difficult to imagine me cutting it in Chilean club land, what with my cagoule, jeans and walking boots. I'm well aware that the men who frequent these establishments fantasise about walking all over the women who work in them, still, I doubt they go quite so obviously attired for it.

The next day the home-from-home vibe persists: a dream of England strained through the grey mist that's blown down from the Andes. Marc and I never have any truck with guides when we're abroad, oh no. We're cool traveller types, not snap-happy tourist ignoramuses. However, we were offered a guide and we've only half a day to cover a lot of ground, so we accepted him.

I'm glad. Ivan Bustamante turns out to be urbane and almost preternaturally wised-up. Besides having the same first name as my second son, he also spent his formative years in Clapham, south London. I kid you not. The Bustamante parents were refugees from Pinochet's regime who ended up living a mile away from my London home. Between 1981 and 1986, Ivan attended Lilian Bayliss, the now notorious local school that the Conservative MP, Oliver Letwin, said he'd rather kill himself than send his child to.

Clearly, Chilean exiles are made of sterner stuff than Tory politicos, because Ivan has turned out very well indeed, leaving school to study music at the University of Croydon, before returning to Santiago in the late 1990s. He tells us he took the job as a city guide so that he could continue with his studies in classical guitar, which isn't any more of an earner in South America than it is in south London.

So, it's off to town, with Ivan discoursing eloquently on everything from constitutional reform, to nineteenth-century urban planning, via detailed statistics of Chilean copper and nitrate production. Squint a little, put my fingers half in my ears, and I could be sitting in an Angus Steakhouse, listening to the Member for Basingstoke. Could've been, except for one thing: on returning to England, I checked up on Mrs Maria Miller. Judging from her Hansard entries, she's a perfectly conscientious Conservative MP, but she has about as much eloquence in English, as I do in menu Spanish. Vote Bustamante! I say.

HANDY ANDES Nº 2. MEAT and TWO VEG.

# Capel-y-Ffin

Sophie is trying to house-train Minnie, a tiny terrier puppy with glossy black fur. So far as I can discern Sophie is a perfect trainer: gentle, yet firm. When Minnie voids one of her mousy little turds on the stone flags of the kitchen, or pees on the settee, Sophie scoops her up, taps her on the nose and says: 'Oooh! You bad girl! How could you? How could you?' They say a dog returns to its own shit (do they? Who are they, and why do they say such things?), but in this case it's me who feels a compulsion to return to writing on the subject: a doleful, incontinent scribe, I am, describing the world with a thick stroke, extruded from my dogged pen.

We're with Bruce and Sophie in the Black Mountains. Bruce doesn't like to travel too much. The last time he went on a low-cost airline was . . . well, the last time he'll ever go. 'I wouldn't have minded if it'd crashed,' he tells me, 'so long as all my fellow passengers died too.'

Such misanthropy isn't easily contained in the built environment, which is why Bruce has retreated here, to the rucked-up folds of westernmost Herefordshire, where glistening polytunnels snake over the fields, as if the Welsh borders were being consumed by an infestation of giant caterpillars designed by the Dr Who props department.

Here, in their fourteenth-century farmhouse, Bruce labours on his magnum opus: a re-evaluation of all values to rival that of Nietzsche. Predictably his preferred writing instrument is an antique IBM golfball electric typewriter, with an early spell-checking gizmo bolted on to it that looks as anachronistic as a sheet of vellum. While Bruce types, Sophie trains Minnie and administers antibiotics to the horse with pneumonia, using a syringe the size of a bicycle pump.

It's a strange set-up – but not half as weird as the one over the hill. I should say 'the one that was over the hill', but the polytunnels have got to me; besides which, the small boys are obsessed by Dr Who at the moment, and every time we get in the car they make Tardis-taking-off noises.

Ten miles over the high, stark range of the Black Mountains, and some eighty years ago, Eric Gill and his extended family arrived at the monastery of Capel-y-Ffin to pursue their experiments in communal living, stone carving and wacky Catholicism. Gill had abandoned his earlier settlement at Ditchling in Sussex, on the grounds that it was too near to town and becoming infected with the spirit of the petit-bourgeoisie.

There was nothing petit-bourgeois about Gill, whose sexual experimentation ran to serial mistresses, troilism, penile etchings, incest, and a smidgeon of paedophilia. In later life Gill's daughters were wont to say that his fiddling about with them during puberty didn't do them any harm at all, but I don't know if the same could be said for the family dog, who couldn't say much about anything. Gill, who kept copious private diaries, recorded his congress with the animal in laconic terms: 'Wondered how P would feel in D' one entry reads; then a further one notes: 'Put P in D'.

Yes, they say a dog always returns to its shit, but I'm equally certain that a sculptor always returns to his bestiality. Even in full sunlight the run-down late-nineteenth-century monastery, where Gill's womenfolk wove rough tunics out of wool-trouvé has a slightly unsettling appearance. It's now a pony trekking centre, and as the small boys and I wander up the valley, we're passed by pony trekkers coming down from the hills. Dumpy little girls auditioning for Thelwell illustrations accompanied by older girls who might be Dr Who's sidekick in some very alternative universe.

The small boys play in the stream, and Luther, the five-year-old, takes possession of a rocky islet he names 'Selfland'. Later on we climb up the side of the range and enter a curious little wood caught in a col. He's overcome by the strangeness of the locale – as well he might be. It's only mid-April but the temperature is in the eighties; the juxtaposition between the heat haze in the valley and the bare branches is quite uncanny. The bracken is tinder-dry, and I wouldn't be that surprised if we came upon the wiry, bearded Gill, wearing his square stone-cutter's hat, folded from a sheet of paper. He may have been the apostle of the everyday erotic, as well as possessing the greatest purity of line of any twentieth-century English artist, but if he were walking his dog I'd run a mile.

As for Luther, he's already well trained in the soiled house of the contemporary world. Looking around him at the woodland he remarks: 'I don't think humans ever come here much – there's no sweet wrappers.'

# On Black Mountain

The Wagon Wheels packet crushed into the damp grass on the slopes of Black Mountain bore a faded illustration of a covered wagon travelling at speed, together with the slogan: 'Size Matters!' Indeed, it does. I was making my way gingerly down this steep hill, which, along with the rest of the massif – from Divis Mountain to Cave Hill – was imagined by Jonathan Swift to be a giant, recumbent figure. Some say that this was his inspiration for the distortions in scale with which he opened *Gulliver's Travels*.

I myself couldn't see it. When I'd flown to Northern Ireland three days previously, my flight into Aldergrove skimmed past Black Mountain to the north, and the day before I'd driven back into town from Fermanagh over a spur of Cave Hill (the supposed nose of the giant). Then, this afternoon, I'd quit my hotel in the centre of town and walked west along the Falls Road. The whole way up this artery – which is imprinted in the national consciousness as the very circulatory system of terror – the landmass loomed above me, its flanks dappled with heather and pitted with old quarry workings. Big it may have been – but anthropoid, not at all.

The last time I was in Belfast it was only shortly after the Easter Accords had been signed, and I walked this way with my friend, the writer Carlo Gébler, then we stomped back into town via the equally notorious Loyalist artery, the Shankhill Road. The time before that it was the early 1990s, and I went up the Falls to visit the Sinn Féin HQ and interview its then Press Officer, Mitchel McLaughlin, who now sits as the Member for South Antrim in the Legislative Assembly.

On neither of those previous occasions do I remember feeling any great anxiety along the Falls, despite the Republican murals of H-block martyrs and gun-wielding paramilitaries; the gun-toting RUC foot patrols and the armoured vehicles swishing past, hopeful 'Crimestoppers' free call numbers painted on their camouflaged sides. But this time it was the May Day bank holiday and the streets were

163

empty; I suspected that if I were to encounter loafing oafs they might well give me a casual, non-sectarian clump. Then, the potential violence was so extreme it was non-apprehensible, now the kids smashing traffic lights with their hurly sticks suggested merely workaday beatings.

At Milltown Cemetery I diverted to visit the IRA plot. It was here, in 1988, that UDA man Michael Stone shot three Republican mourners at a funeral. Three days later two British Army corporals, who accidentally ran into the funeral for one of these victims, were dragged from their car, beaten by the crowd and then summarily executed. So the Troubles eked themselves out in grotesque dribs and drabs of human life, adding up to 3,500 in all.

Even on a bright day, with sun and showers alternating, there remained something minatory about Milltown. A couple of tight-faced street drinkers loitered among the overgrown Victorian graves. The IRA plot is like an ancient chamber tomb: the volunteers' black marble markers arranged in a boat-shaped compound, while at the prow the declaration of the 1916 Easter Rising is carved in stone.

I turned my back on the city and trudged up the Monagh bypass, then past the travellers' camp and along the Upper Springfield Road. Finally I reached open ground and headed on up to the ridge. Public access to the Black Mountain has only been possible for the last couple of years, before that the British Army held sway up here: they still have a huge listening post on the summit of Divis.

The evening before I'd met a warden for the new park that's being created here, and he told me that the hills were becoming well-used by the city's inhabitants. This didn't accord with my experience: as the wind soughed over the heather I saw only a posse of traveller kids coursing for hares, their tracksuits flapping as they ran after their lurchers. And the heather itself was burnt to a crisp, while fresh yellow blades of grass speared between the scorched roots. The same warden had told me that the kids set fire to the heather every year, and that really it wasn't such a bad thing, since it provided one of the few remaining habitats suitable for the red grouse to nest in.

It was beautiful up on the hills, with achingly long views south-west to Strangford Lough, and over thirty miles south to the conical Mountains of Mourne. In the near distance, on the far side of town, I could make out the pale, stone monstrosity of Stormont: a Brobdingnagian parliament built for politicians all too often fit only for Lilliput. The following day would see Tony Blair and Bertie Ahern descend on Stormont to celebrate the new devolved Government of the Democratic Unionists and Sinn Féin with plenty of mutual back-slapping.

But the arrival of these giants lay in the future; for the meantime it was I who was slapping the back of the mighty hill with my boots. Immediately below me I could see the enclaves of Ballymurphy and Springmartin, still separated by thirty-foot-high 'peace walls' topped by razor wire, and I wondered, which one would it be safer to walk through, the Big or the Little Endians?

# So Long Toulouse

In *Moulin Rouge*, John Huston's 1951 biopic of the French painter and absinthe-bucket, Henri Toulouse-Lautrec, José Ferrer played the lead – entirely on his knees. The action begins in a Parisian bar, Toulouse-Lautrec sits supping his deathly-green mouthwash – the barman polishes the glasses. Then the painter clambers down off his stool. Suddenly we're in his POV, looking up at the great zinc-topped escarpment of the counter; the barman leans over, peers down at us, and speaks the first line of the movie: 'So long, Toulouse!'

I resolved to walk to Toulouse in the spirit of Ferrer's Oscar-winning performance: by which I mean, that for large portions of the journey I would be semi-recumbent on trains. First I would walk from my home in Stockwell, south London, to the Eurostar Terminal at Waterloo Station, then I'd entrain for the Gare du Nord. In Paris, I would stump across town to the Gare Montmartre and entrain once more for the far south.

In Toulouse, I would walk to my hotel, walk to the theatre where I was giving a reading with the chanteuse Marianne Faithfull, walk to dinner, limp to bed, and in the morning I'd do the whole thing in reverse: a nice weekend's stroll, covering some 1,300 miles. My wife, ever sceptical of these peregrinations, always says the same thing: 'Will you walk up and down the train?' She refuses to accept the musicality of my giant steps, their alternation of rhythmic striding and the fermata of the rail compartment.

The night before I left I ran into Bobby. He got the Toulouse walk. He grew up in Florida and used to water-ski across the Everglades, from lake to lake, his transit linking the Atlantic seaboard and the Gulf of Mexico. 'We'd stop at amazing restaurants to eat fried chicken and gumbo.'

It was a dullish morning in London and rain threatened. Down by the Vauxhall railway arches the late-night revellers at Fire were punching the air, trying to KO

the new day. Along the Albert Embankment, it was debatable that earth had not anything to show more fair. On the 6.37 a.m. train to Paris, the stewardess was chatty: they're moving the terminal to St Pancras and it'll make her trip to the trip that's work a grinding urban commute. It will render my walking tours of Paris equally unappealing, with all that London to march through before I reach the Boulevard de Magenta. The sixty kilometres through the Channel Tunnel has been walked, of course – by a thirty-six year old Russian in 1998. But he was on his way to join the Foreign Legion and not officially sanctioned, a fugitive, on his knees – metaphorically – and what fun is that?

Aeolus was tossing buckets against the train windows in England – and then in France. But the drizzle was light as I strode away from the Gare du Nord, making for the Seine. I'd eschewed the map to give myself the delusion I knew my way around – or, perhaps, to make the walk seem more like a Situationist's aimless *dérive*. I cut off Magenta before the Boulevard de Strasbourg and headed south down Rue Faubourg St Denis. As ever with these intermittent walks, the two cities had been kicked into one by my boots: London was exoticised – while Paris seemed ineffably mundane. I liked that. I liked the way the Porte de Denis had all the historical resonance of a five-bar gate. Naturally I got lost around Les Halles, but then recovered myself to saunter across the Pont Neuf, through Saint-Germain and up the Rue de Rennes. A swift espresso, priced at six euros, and it was into the uglification of the Gare Montmartre.

In Toulouse I left the station and headed along the Boulevard Pierre Sémard, which bordered a canal, then turned down the Allée Jean Jaurès, a wide, dull boulevard that debouched into the charming little Place Wilson, where I found a grandiose monument to the Occitan poet Pierre Goudouli. Ah, French urban place names! Where else in the world can you go from martyred Communist trade union leader, to socialist premier to US president, all within forty minutes. I trod on along the revolutionary Frenchman who was the US's greatest friend – Rue Lafayette – until I reached the Place Capitole and checked into the Crown-Plaza.

That evening, at dinner in a brasserie on the Place Wilson, my friend François Ravard told me of the amazing sight he had witnessed that afternoon: a float of Gay Pride marchers being drawn through Toulouse by a melancholy French peasant sporting an Asterix moustache and driving a tractor. Meanwhile, another of our fellow diners informed us that the Charlemagne Regiment (a French division of the Waffen SS) were holding their annual reunion in a town an hour's drive west of Toulouse. Such strange ambulatory antics! They made my own homage to José Ferrer seem positively banal.

# Epitaph for a Small Loser

Let me offer you my latest travels, which consisted of a 15,000-mile sweep through the Americas, North and South, that produced a series of giant carbon footprints, while giving me hardly any opportunity to stretch my legs. I blame the kids: two small boys are a sufficient drogue to brake any possibility of sustained walking, unless it's on a treadmill facing a marathon screening of all the Harry Potter movies.

*Walk 1: São Paulo Airport.* Distance: 260 metres. Time: 2.5 hours.

Don't be fooled by the comparatively short distances and level terrain into thinking that this will be an easy hike. Consisting of four separate stages: Domestic Transfers Check-in Desk; TAM Ticketing Desk; TAM Check-in and Security, the walk – or 'queue' as it is colloquially known – can become especially arduous if you undertake it, as we did, in the immediate aftermath of a strike by Brazilian air traffic controllers. We flew in at 6.30 a.m. in a daze, but by the time we'd been 'walking' for three hours, we *knew* where we were. Purgatory.

*Walk 2: From the head of the funicular to the base of the statue of Christ the Redeemer.* Distance: 200 metres. Time, including refreshment stop: 1 hour.

Everyone, just everyone, has to visit this huge statue when they come to Rio. It's just *so* huge, and the views from the top of the mountain are superb. At least, they are on clear days. On the one we attempted our trek it was so cloudy we could see neither up nor down. The youngest of our party did exclaim 'Oh my God!' when he saw the vast Redeemer looming out of the mist, but while this may have been apt, he is also – being five – utterly credulous.

*Walk 3: Copacabana to Ipanema.* Distance: 1.5 kilometres. Time: 2 hours.

Put all thoughts of Astrud Gilberto and the eponymous girl out of your mind. Beachfront Rio may no longer have been quite as threatening as when I was last here, in the early 1990s, but being winter it was still a misty, chilly, slightly scuzzy prospect, as the author's wife never ceased to remind him.

The boys liked to walk up the beach – which, to be fair, is pristine – then back down the Avenida Atlantica, time after time after time. Eventually, I persuaded them to divert up the Rua Francesco Otavacano to Ipanema, past a scary Catholic iconostasis (life-size plaster figures of leprous-looking saints). It was dark by the time we turned into the Avenida Francesco Behring, and there was absolutely no one on the beach at all. The breakers rolled in from the Atlantic, and the lights of the hilly suburbs to the south mounted up as if Christ the Redeemer were developing the empyrean itself.

Towards the end of the point was the Parque Garota. The author's wife felt that its dark shrubbery and sinister-sounding appellation disqualified it as a location for family rambling, but I pointed out that 'garota' is in fact 'girl' in Portuguese, and the park was named after the eponymous one. 'In that case,' Mrs Self snapped, 'why is it full of single men lurking in the bushes?'

*Walk 4: Paraty, Brazil. Round trip from the Marquesa Hotel.* Distance: 2 kilometres. Time: 1.5 hours.

If you visit the charming seaside resort of Paraty, three and a half hours' drive north of Rio, be sure to tour its famously uneven, large-cobbled streets on foot. The grid-pattern of boxy, whitewashed houses will be familiar to anyone who has ever seen a spaghetti western.

Abandoning the boys at the hotel, I acquired sturdy walking companions, to whit: the entire staff of the British Council office in Rio de Janeiro, together with a journalist from *Il Globo*, his photographer, and the jeep they'd all hired.

I asked them why they were on my case, they explained that they'd paid my plane fare to the literary festival that was being held in Paraty, and they wanted their face time. This was all news to me, I don't like having anything to do with Council, which is an adjunct of the Foreign Office, charged with converting the heathen to reruns of *The Vicar of Dibley*. They wanted to go for a drive – I insisted on walking. I prevailed, and we set out for the jetty where the pleasure boats are hired, the whole media cavalcade stringing along behind.

The journalist asked me questions, his snapper snapped away. The head of the British Council and I chatted amiably enough. (It's impossible to do anything else with them, as Holly Martins discovered in The *Third Man*, when he encountered the BC rep, Crabbin, memorably played by the late Wilfrid Hyde-White.) We made it to the jetty, and then after further excruciating politeness, I managed to shake them off. Bliss.

# Doggerland de Nos Jours

Consider Doggerland, the landmass that before the end of the last ice age connected the British Isles with the Netherlands, Denmark and Germany.

My brother wised me up on Doggerland, sitting in the humid garden of his house in upstate New York: 'When we think of Britain and the continent being connected we obviously imagine an isthmus or land bridge,' he averred, 'whereas the reality was an enormous plain. Archaeologists have discovered human artefacts and evidence of habitations from the Mesolithic in this area. Think of it! A tundra where the North Sea is now, teeming with game – lion, mammoth, hippo – crisscrossed by the trails of sophisticated huntsmen.'

I thought on it for a while then I flew home to London, smirching the sky with more than my fair share of cosmic lamp blacking. Back in town the heavens opened and the rains came down like stair rods – except that no one under forty was in a position to employ this simile, because they've never seen a stair rod in their lives.

A puddle formed in the back garden five feet across – this was unprecedented. The small boys' school was closed due to flooding, and I went to pick them up on the bicycle, then, three-up, we toured the local wet spots. The low points of Silverthorne and Queenstown Roads were flooded: scuzzy meres with kerbstone banks and littorals defined by police incident tape.

The small boys were excited by this inversion of the normal state of things. You don't spend two years of your young lives with your dad upstairs typing a futuristic, dystopic novel about flooded Britain for nothing. We discussed the possibilities of London being seriously inundated, and foolishly I gave it to them straight: Yes, I thought it was definitely rather than maybe, to adapt an album title from the aptly named beat combo, Oasis. Predictably, the small boys grew anxious, and began discussing among themselves what toys could be saved.

Returning home, I thought of my friends in the Vale of Pershore – we were due to go up for the weekend; usually, we all indulge in a little wild-water swimming in the Avon, but this water was going to be way too wild for that. It wasn't long before the sewers of rolling TV began to back up with the breaking flood news. I called up to see how they were doing: 'We're cut off,' Charles said. 'But the most bizarre thing is that Gabriel has been watching the Test at Lord's all afternoon, where there's bright sunshine.'

Yes, after all, the paradigm for the deluge remains Genesis Chapters 6–10. It's a short tale – with a powerful resonance. The main facts are well known: God, an irascible super-being, prone to creating marvellous things, but afflicted with severe Attention Deficit Disorder, gives life to humanity, but then gets quickly bored with it: 'And it repented the Lord that he had made man on the earth, and it grieved him at his heart.'

The solution was obvious: lay on forty days and forty nights of stair rods (although the simile is questionable, since although 'there were giants in the earth in those days' (Gen. 6: 4), they had yet to invent the stair carpet, or even the run-ner), then instruct a morally recondite sex-centenarian to build a fuck-off big boat in order to preserve breeding pairs of all genotypes (except insects, which were invented by Beelzebub in 1923).

The important thing here is that the standard account of the antediluvian – which every morally recondite son of the manse, such as our own Prime Minister, well knows – is that the ignorant, the venal and the lazy get it in the neck (the water, that is), while the Good are saved, so that when the dove pitches up they're in pole position to build enormous towers on the floodplains, and invest in the booming language school business that soon comes into being. It's obvious that the Prime Minister subscribes to this view. Touring Gloucester shortly after it went 'glub-glub', he referred time and again to the exceptional nature of the rainfall. If he didn't have an overwhelmingly secular electorate, the words 'Act of God' would've shot through his lips.

But from where I'm sitting it's Britain's Sodoms and Gomorrahs that remained high and dry, while the likes of my friend Charles had his livelihood all but trashed. His crops were washed away, his barns soaked, and the Poles who come every summer to do the picking (most of whom are professors of theology), ended up paddling. Still, what the tide brings in the tide takes out again. I expect there were seasonal workers in Doggerland (in the Mesolithic they favoured transhu-manance), and when it became impossible, due to rising sea levels, to walk home to Poland, they, too, took it personally.

# Cardinism

'Today I made the ascent of the highest mountain in this region, which is not improperly called Ventosum. My only motive was the wish to see what so great an elevation had to offer. I have had the expedition in mind for many years . . .' so begins Petrarch's justly celebrated account of his ascent of Mont Ventoux, a peak at the west end of the Luberon massif in Provence.

Luberon. Mm . . . The very region *sounds* lubricious, to me. It makes me think of dallying with libidinous Cathars in valleys rather than climbing up 2,000 metres of bare limestone-capped mountain. But then Petrarch was made of sterner stuff. 'Remorseless toil,' he observed, 'conquers all.' He claimed that his 1336 hike was the first taken since antiquity purely in order to admire the view. Others have disputed this – as well they might. Founding father of Humanism Petrarch may have been – Norris McWhirter he wasn't.

Besides, his account is studded with spiritual exhortations; you can't imagine Janet Street-Porter coming out with: 'The life we call blessed is sought for in a high eminence, and strait is the way that leads to it.' Nor, I imagine, do most of us always have a copy of Augustine's *Confessions* on hand when we go hill walking, to liberally quote from should we feel the impulse.

Still, there I was, in the Luberon, and while climbing Mont Ventoux seemed a little *de trop*, I still had an urge to get out in that maquis and deprive Jean of his source (or is it Manon?). Why shouldn't I scale the Petit Luberon, a lesser limestone escarpment to the south of Mont Ventoux? And why not provide myself with a motivation to match Petrarch's own lack of one?

The village of Lacoste suggested itself as a starting point (suggested . . . it always strikes me as such a *suggestible* word), because the Marquis de Sade lived here, and his castle still stands on the hilltop, a suitably medieval-looking ruin, in this landscape fractured by religious schism: Protestant against Catholic, Catholic

SAINT AUGUSTINE RECLINING — CHAPTER and VERSE...

Ralph STEADman 2007

against Protestant, and everyone against the libidinous Cathars.

Daytime temperatures were hitting 37 degrees, and August isn't really the month for strenuous exertion in this part of the world – not that the locals see it that way: the day before I set out a cycle race climbed the zigzag road to Lacoste, its Lycra-clad, tight-shirted contestants looking – from behind – more than ready to embark on 120 days of Sodom. Poor Tommy Simpson, the English cyclist, was done for by the heat when he pumped his way to the top of Mont Ventoux during the 1967 Tour de France. Granted, there were amphetamines and alcohol found in his bloodstream, but who among us can honestly claim that we've never cycled up a mountain pissed and speeding? While for the Tour, it's always: *Plus ça change.*

I elected – like Petrarch – to leave before dawn, and by the time the sunlight was streaming down through the trees I was already high up on the Petit Luberon, with de Sade's castle well below and behind me. At the top of the escarpment the rocky path levelled out and I entered the mysterious Forêt des Cèdres. Actually, there was nothing mysterious about this at all – it was a forest of cedars: big, shaggy trees, their foliage trailing on the ground. It seemed I'd narrowly missed out on a herd of Eeyores, because everywhere were rude shelters built from fallen boughs.

Then, as I reached the far side of the plateau, and the massif fell away from me in successive lower peaks carpeted with thorny scrub, it hit me: I would devise a latter-day perversion to match any ever dreamed of by Donatien Alphonse-François de Sade. It was this that would provide my motivation as my feet stumbled on the sharp limestone outcrops, this noble pursuit that would be my trailblazer as I joined the Grande Randonée down into the valley.

It worked: meditating hard on what I might get up to, given two cyclists, a copy of Augustine's *Confessions* and a large saucisson sec, I motored past the lonely 'Peak of the Eagles' and down towards the turning point of my trek, Le Tapis. I checked to see if there were any children down the well, then turned back, marvelling at the way the escarpment high overhead had been eroded by run-off into fantastical arches, spires, and an exact likeness of Gérard Depardieu.

By the time I was heading once more down the rocky track towards Lacoste (as Petrarch would have it: 'a heavy body weighed down by members'), my own salacious feverishness was greater than the air temperature: someone had told me that de Sade's castle was now the property of the octogenarian designer Pierre Cardin, and he was in the process of transforming it into a comfy bourgeois home. Perhaps cardinism was the perversion I sought? And what is cardinism? I hear you ask. Simple: sexual relief obtained by castle conversions. This may be an expensive way of getting your jollies, but with the housing market the way it is . . .

# Bring Me the Villa of Alfredo Garcia

'The villa,' Marc remarks magniloquently, 'is like something that might have been designed by the bastard offspring of Gianni Versace and Saddam Hussein.' It's worse than pedantic to point out that this is a biological impossibility, because the villa definitely does look like precisely this; and if it can exist, then why not the love-architect of the dress designer and the dictator?

The villa is surmounted by an oculus studded with enough stones for a thousand rockeries. The rooms are white and red with heavy wooden beams. The entrance hall – white marble floor, natch – is dominated by a Moorish fountain. There are ashtrays like chandeliers and chandeliers like ashtrays. There are silky sofas the colour of semi-precious stones in abundance. An enormous bull's head is nailed to a plaque high up on the kitchen wall; you might be tempted to slice carpaccio off it – if you were insane. The outbuildings are faux-adobe, the gardens are full of palms and Dr Seuss-style exercises in topiary. The pool points south, towards Ibiza town, where the bastion of the Crusader castle, topped by the eighteenth-century cathedral, dominates the skyline.

Everyone gets the villa they deserve, on this, the most mutable and hallucinogenic of isles. The lotus eaters slob out by the pool, cuddling with Circe, while I keep expecting a wealthy Mexican to thrust his dishonoured daughter in my face and order me to bring him the head of Alfredo Garcia. Meanwhile, Warren Oates crouches in the pool house, cooing to a bloody lump in a hessian sack. We eat lunch within a loggia, talking of ingesting MDMA rectally and the foibles of the Great Powers. Wasps swarm on the lumps of chicken and beef we've left for them, then, too obese to sting, they blade-hop back to their subterranean nest in the rockery by the pool.

When night falls, we leap into our Chrysler MPVs and race in convoy through the faux-adobe towns and the parched hillocks of the hinterland, to where tempo-

179

FAUX FUN

rary car park attendants wave torches, assigning Porsches and Ferraris to the dusty ditch. We debouch, and follow soused starlets, tottering like newborn foals on high-hoofs, into parties organised for friendless internet billionaires by unpopular retail millionaires. Barmen mix mojitos with all the time in the world, while you wait in a queue of hair care product tycoons and Russian wives-by-the-hour. A man taps you on the shoulder: he once sold you a shirt, in Soho, in the last millennium.

Ah! Ibiza, with your infinity pools and your retiree dancers who're convinced they'll jig for ever! Ah! Ibiza, with your congealed beaches and your foamy dance floors – who could not love you, such is your sybaritic honesty, your wilful disregard for any culture save club. The charter jets take off all through the dark nights, carrying gel-heads back to the K-holes of Manchester, Leeds and Birmingham! Who can fail to wax lyrical – or even just wax.

One afternoon my daughter and I walk up to the old town, penetrating the sixty-foot-thick walls of the bastion. We stroll through the narrow streets of the old medina, past cafés and tourist tat-shops. A Hassidic man stands on a balcony dressed in black; small leather boxes containing verses of a holy book are tied to his forehead and his upper arm, he rocks back and forth, sing-speaking his creed. He wouldn't look out of place in Privilege or DC9 – but what's he doing here?

Another morning, and suffering a tad from claustrophobia, I drive up to the north, in search of the wilder side of Ibiza. But if this is wild – Regent's Park is the Yukon. True, the hills are a little higher, and the villas are a bit more spaced out, but you still sense that behind every 'Privado' sign there lurks a Milanese bra manufacturer with too much time on his hands.

My nine-year-old and I tramp along four kilometres of dusty blacktop, between drowsy olive groves. Finally, the road loops down through five-metre-high stands of bamboo to a rocky inlet. At last, after the teeming streets of Eivissa and Sant Antoni, and the choked beaches of D'en Bossa and Beniràss, there is no one; or rather, only a fat Frenchman, who squats naked beside some fishermen's huts – and that's as good as no one.

We disrobe and inch our way into the waters. True they aren't possessed of the deep clarity of the Prime Minister's political thinking – but nor are they brown. We splash for a few seconds, then we are both stung by jellyfish. Nursing our electrified limbs we retreat to the rocks, where the Frenchman lazily observes: 'Thees side of the cove is, owewesai? Full of the medusas . . .'

But his warning is way too late, because once more that greater Gorgon, Ibiza, is in our sights: the snakes writhe above her Dolce & Gabbana sunglasses, and we're turned . . . to stone.

# Thirteen Million Candle Power

Glencoe. It's late August but already there's a hint of autumn in the air, along with the droplets of smirr and the midges dancing between them. Further south the heather is still in full flower, but up here in the central Highlands, the stark triangles of the mountains are at first tawny, then swathed in grey mist, then tawny again. I unload the car and pitch the tent, while the small boys head off to explore the riverbank. I want them to fetch firewood, but they return empty-handed: over the summer the campsite has been picked clean, bucolic louts have even hacked at the living alders and birches.

I head off downstream to where some large timber has been disgorged on to the stony bluffs. It's too large: entire trees, their root systems embedded with rocks, lie like stranded krakens. I wrench a couple of limbs off and drag them back, then gather a few handfuls of twigs and wager our last firelighters on stimulating a con-flagration. Dusk and clouds are flowing down into the U-shaped glacial valley, the midges are getting fierce: we need smoke.

Then comes Colin. I've encountered him already, a portly, middle-aged man, in grey tracksuit bottoms and a check wool shirt. He has a regulation bald patch, and as I passed him on the path he wished me a cheery 'Good evening' in a New World accent that I couldn't place. Now he comes up to our fireplace and says, 'I heard the kids' voices and had to come over, I'm missing my own ones and dying for a little company,' then he giggles, a disagreeable cartoon chuckle. 'I was sitting at home in Glasgow at 6 a.m. this morning, when I decided that I couldn't stand the city any more, so I got in the car and drove up here,' again the naughty giggle and a conspiratorial look. I came here to get away from *all* Colins, but this one has latched on effortlessly.

'I don't think that's gonna catch,' he says, gesturing at the fire. It's true. The early promise of the firelighters has given way to a forlorn charring. 'I've got some

kindling and logs in the car, if your lad'll give me a hand,' he gestures at my nine-year-old, selecting his volunteer, 'I'll go and get them.'

'Go on then, Ivan,' I say, but as he obediently trots off through the woodland behind Colin I am gripped by a dreadful anxiety: this Colin isn't just some saddo loner with grating mannerisms, he's a highly organised paedophile, who's going to whip my son into the back of his car and drive him away . . . Glencoe will become the ominous backdrop for another bloody massacre . . . Then I check myself: Christ! I'm falling victim to just the free-ranging stranger-danger paranoia I so despise in the commonality; I'm damning a man for a pervert simply because he's being friendly. I hunker down to the fire, trying to coax it back into life – but it's no good, the anxious worm is boring through me, and I find myself scampering through the woodland in studiedly casual pursuit, only to encounter Colin and Ivan on their way back with the logs.

So, having falsely accused him, I'm condemned to Colin for the evening. Still suspicious I draw him out. It's a rule of meetings with unremarkable men, that if you question them, they'll remain transfixed by their own incuriosity. So it is with Colin. While we get the fire going (and even with his logs, his coal and his kindling, it fails to properly ignite until he applies his electric air pump), and the boys toast their marshmallows and slurp their hot chocolate, I learn a lot about him, while he remains in total ignorance of us.

Colin's parents emigrated to Canada when he was a kid. He grew up there, joined the Canadian Navy, trained as a radar plotter, then left and came back to his native Scotland in the early 1990s. He hasn't worked properly since. He has a girlfriend and a couple of kids. He's also got diabetes and has had five heart attacks. I'm shocked when he tells me he's four years younger than me – he looks much older. He sits at home in Glasgow, growing hydroponic weed in his cupboard, which explains the giggling and the claustrophobia. Every so often he drives his Mondeo up north and squats in this campsite, staring out at the mountains he's incapable of climbing.

As I pump Colin for his life story a sadness emerges that blankets Glencoe quite as thickly as the darkness. Even when he gets out the 13-million-candle-power torch he bought at Argos for £29.99 it fails to dispel my gloom: this is just a cock-up of a man, no conspirator. Eventually, the small boys are asleep on their rug by the fire, and Colin takes his leave: 'I've got my laptop in the tent,' he tells me proudly. 'I'm gonna watch *The Da Vinci Code*.'

# Dum-Dum
# Want Gum Gum

I couldn't leave you this year without saying a little bit about my trip to Easter Island in February with the artist Marc Quinn. Quinn, who is perhaps best known for his sculpture of his own head, using his own frozen blood, is a dry, witty companion to have on a long-haul, multi-time-zone journey. We hit on the idea of going to Easter Island while we were staying on Ibiza in the summer of 2006, and both read Jared Diamond's excellent survey of failed civilisations, *Collapse*.

Diamond's account of the rise and fall of this, the most extraordinary Polynesian society, on the remotest inhabited island in the world, may not be the most authoritative – but he takes you there: into the dark hearts of a people doomed by their own competitive sculpture building. Broad-brush fantasists such as Thor Heyerdahl and Erich von Däniken may have used the famous moai, or standing stone statues of Easter Island, to bolster their own weird theories about human migrations and origins, but the painstaking archaeology of the last half-century has revealed a truth even more bizarre.

Arriving some time in the sixth century, the Rapanuians (the natives' name for themselves and their home) discovered a thickly wooded, lush jewel of an island that they speedily set about cultivating. Eight hundred years later, it's estimated that the original 150-odd settlers had burgeoned into 10,000 or more. Along with the vast population – Rapanui is only fifteen miles long – came massive resource-depletion. The original tree cover of giant palms was chopped down to make the scaffolding required for the carving of the moai, the runners and 'roads' needed for their movement and erection.

The moai themselves were portraiture: stylised depictions of once-living elders, erected on 'ahu' or ceremonial platforms, so that they might watch over the doings of their descendants. And what doings they were, gripped by the building of bigger and bigger moai (there's one only half-hacked out of the quarry at Hanga Roa that

would've stood twenty metres high and weighed 200 tons), the Rapanuians ended up chopping down all the trees. They were then unable to build the big outriggers needed for deep-sea fishing – and the island itself could no longer support them.

Civil war and anarchy were already under way when the white man pitched up and hastened the destruction with guns, germs and steel. Within decades all that was left were the toppled statues and a few score deracinated natives. There was a moral here – as well as some fabulous statuary – although it's debatable whether it's one that could be appreciated simply by visiting the place. After all, although a designated World Heritage Sight – whatever that means – going to Easter Island is a double-edged paradox for the environmentally concerned of such sharpness that it threatens to chop your psyche in two.

On the one hand, if we don't visit the island, the Rapanuians, who have re-colonised the place after being dragged off into slavery by Peruvians and Chileans in the nineteenth century, will be doomed to a second extinction, as they depend solely on the tourist trade. But on the other hand, the twenty hours of carbon-shitting flight from Europe, and the heavy tread of injection-moulded, high-tech Gore-Tex boots around the sacred sites, are inexorably completing the job begun by the status-obsessed moai builders themselves.

As Marc and I traversed half the known world, we began to run across moai that had been exiled from paradise: or rather, concrete travesties of the statues that contained within their cartoonish features a doomy warning. There was a moai on a traffic island in Santiago, there were the massed ranks of the knick-knack moai on the island itself: political prisoners of the tourist economy. Then, when we returned to England, I began to see vulgarised moai wherever I looked. There were a few sunk in the shark tank at the London Aquarium, a couple more on sale at the antiques centre near my parents-in-law's house in Lanarkshire, and then, finally, there were the moai outside the themed 'South Sea' bar on Kennington Road, only half a mile from where I live.

Could it be that these gimcrack copies are, in some quirk of the space-time continuum, effigies of my own ancestors, dropped down in sarf London to keep an eye on my own destructive tendencies? Marc himself drew my attention to the kiddie film Night at the Museum, in which the exhibits at the Natural History Museum in New York come to life, including a giant moai that dubs itself 'Dum-Dum'. Dum-Dum's catchphrase is 'Dum-Dum wants gum gum,' and the horror of this shtick is that it isn't the Easter Island statues that are dumb, but us: speechless in the face of our own consuming desire to chew up the earth, and every last little bit of latex in it.

# Grisly, man

Ralph claims that this picture faithfully reproduces a life-threatening encounter that he had with a grizzly bear during his most recent sojourn in Canada. According to Ralph, he drove the devilish bear off with his ink pot. It's all lies, of course. I know because I've just been in Canada and I heard the whole story from several eye-witnesses who saw Ralph and the Grizzly together.

So, it's not that Ralph was entirely deluded; on the contrary it was inevitable that he would meet up with a grizzly sooner or later, as with global warming disrupting the environment of the far north, the ranges of the former (*Artificer cantankerous*) and the latter (*Ursus arctos horribilis*) increasingly overlap. We've all read tales of troublesome grizzlies venturing into North American cities and pestering their inhabitants with visceral and disturbing graphic works. Most of us probably considered what might happen when the two species met up – although no one anticipated that they would fall in love.

I don't know why Ralph is so coy about his inter-specific love affair with Griselda (for such, I have ascertained, is the name of 'his' bear), because the previous year, during his time at the Harbourfront Festival in Toronto, the two of them were inseparable. Jim, the driver for the Festival (he says 'Hello', Ralph, by the way), picked them up together at the airport and drove them into town.

For the next three days, except when Ralph was required onstage at the Festival, he and Griselda were shacked up in Room 2146. Neither bear nor artist were seen to mingle with the other authors who were gathered in the hospitality suite on the penthouse floor – leading them to suspect that Ralph was being huffy and stand-offish.

All except Kazuo Ishiguro, who came upon Ralph and Griselda swimming together in the hotel pool. 'To be honest,' he told me recently, 'I was a little bit fried. I'd pulled an all-nighter with Margaret Atwood. We got pissed and she used

this computerised "long pen" device that she's invented to sign books at remote locations, to, ah, y'know, pinch people's bottoms in European bookshops and otherwise generally molest them. It was childish behaviour, and I'm not that proud of myself. Anyway, I thought I'd sober up with a sauna at around 6 a.m., and went down to the spa on the fifth floor. There were these two enormous bear-like figures frolicking together in the pool . . .

'They seemed very affectionate. Steadman was sort of lifting the bear out of the water and tossing it about – or, as they say in Canada, "aboot" – and from time to time he'd twang the strap of its bikini top. I was amazed, because I'd been for a swim in the pool myself, and the chlorine was so strong that I'd spent the next four hours half-blinded, yet neither Steadman nor the bear seemed in the least discomfited.'

'Discomfited', eh? I think the use of that very term alone confirms this indisputably as the authentic testimony of the Booker prize-winning author. But if any further verification were needed, we have the copies of Ralph's room-service bills at the Westin Harbour. In three days, Room 2146 ordered up twenty-seven club sandwiches, eighteen cheeseburgers, twenty-seven porterhouse steaks, seventeen full breakfasts – and even requested the concierge that he simply 'bring the goddam wheelie-bin up from the kitchen'.

It's fair to say that Canada is no longer the society it once was. Gone are the days when the entire culture was crimped by a dour – if polite – Presbyterianism, and sexual activity of any kind whatsoever was frowned upon. Nowadays, the Conservative Premier, Stephen Harper, is often seen at state banquets completely naked save for a strategically placed maple leaf and with a very fetching beaver on his arm. Canadians explain their re-evaluation of all values with reference to the changing climate – it never freezes anymore – and the high rate of immigration: Calgary is now the biggest Brazilian city in the world. In the US, those mad Manicheans would've put a stop to Ralph's goings-on, but such was the atmosphere of tolerance in Toronto, that he returned in September of this year, hoping to rekindle his passion. Only to discover that Griselda had run away with a Major League hockey player, whose build was more to her taste. Hence Ralph's defamatory drawing, and wish-fulfilment fantasy – the work of both a demented and a rejected suitor.

# Whistlin' in Sausalito

'When I see a guy lighting a goddam cigarette as I come round the corner, I see a guy who ain't taking the bus into town!' exclaims the bus driver, a competent black woman, who even as I feed my four one-dollar bills into the machine, is ramming the big whooshing box up the ramp on to Route 101, heading north for San Francisco. 'City of Industry' is the slogan picked out in big white letters on the hillside ahead – presumably it's some sort of riposte to 'HOLLYWOOD', but I doubt the Los Angelenos can read it at this distance.

It's pointless to explain to the bus driver that this is a guy who's down to three cigarettes a day, after a lifetime spent flying around inside a blue-brown cloud. In the past I've animadverted on the way the space-time continuum is graduated by smoking, but now I'm down to three the shifts are dizzying: I was last embodied in dank Toronto, then I winked out of existence for a few hours, before being beamed down a white paper tube into smouldering California.

I'm absurdly happy. I may not be undertaking my favourite form of airport transit – walking – but I have eschewed the cab, and that has to be a good thing. Cabs suck: they're the real culprits when it comes to urban disorientation. You aren't merely hiring a car and driver when you step into a cab – you're hiring the cabby's local geographical nous. No matter how hard you try to concentrate on where he's taking you, you still end up subsiding into foggy supposition: this is somewhere you don't know, and he's going the long way round this agglomeration of ignorance.

But take the bus, and the mere act of finding the stop, looking at the route map, and then negotiating your way from the city centre stop to your hotel, will begin to make things legible. Dusk is falling as I turn the corner into Market Street, and I'm still happy to be reading the city, so happy that I swerve into a bookstore and buy a copy of *Great Expectations*, because I'm certain I have them.

FAIL TODAY — GONE TOMORROW

The following morning the weather is set fair, and I resolve to walk to Sausalito. It'll be a modest enough twelve-miler from downtown San Francisco, dog-legging over the Golden Gate Bridge. Of course, I don't have a topographic map, and although Nob Hill is in my face, I can't find a way round it. I slave up the famously vertiginous streets, listening to the chains of the funiculars rattling beneath my feet. By the time I reach the North Point I feel like Herbie in *The Love Bug*. My bonnet is flapping, my oil is leaking.

It's Sunday and the esplanade is thronged with walkers, joggers, bikers, crackpot preachers, and those ubiquitous denizens of American cities – in many ways their most typical inhabitants – the homeless, who have been tossed by the rampaging bull of commercialism, and compelled to wander the streets pushing shopping carts piled high with their fucked-up chattels. I bet they know where they are, though.

Up on the bridge there are still more walkers. Indeed, it occurs to me that this is more ambulatory activity than I've ever seen anywhere in the States before – except Manhattan. Perhaps this is what Americans need to galvanise them: something really big – but man-made – to walk over. Halfway across there are emergency phones advertising: 'Crisis Counseling' (sic). 'There is Hope. Make the Call. The Consequences of Jumping from this Bridge are Fatal and Tragic.'

The 'tragic' is a nice touch, no? It places even the most commonplace suicide on a set of monumental proportions, enacting a Götterdämmerung of awesome scale, leaping from between the very strings of this monumental lyre, as Aeolus himself strums them. But then again, presumably that's why the most commonplace suicides are drawn to the Golden Gate, and the 'tragic', far from dissuading them, is likely to be the final confirmation of the rightness of their actiooooooooon!

Grim thoughts dog me as I double back under the end of the bridge, then trudge through the precincts of a coastguard station and on into Sausalito, where the houses are more shingled than anything has a right to be – unless it actually has shingles. There are these wooden excrescences, then there are the gift shops selling china knick-knacks and T-shirts, and 'art' galleries shoving hideous daubs in my face.

I slurp down a dozen indifferent oysters at Spinnaker's on the quayside. Dusk is falling across the bay. I feel moderately satisfied: at least I know where I am, even if the woman at the next table is having a nervous breakdown, sobbing noisily into her clam chowder. On the ferry back to San Francisco the day-trippers light up the night sky with their camera flashes as we cruise past Alcatraz, imprisoning the empty penitentiary in their steely little boxes. Forever.

# Horned Helmet

On a recent plane flight from Heathrow Airport, London to Glasgow, I entered into a typical – but for all that grindingly depressing – altercation. I had been assigned the window seat, while the aisle was occupied by a man two decades younger and a head and a half shorter than myself. I pointed this out to him and suggested that he might have some compassion for his elder, taller, better; but he demurred, saying that he wanted to 'get out quickly' at our destination. 'What are you,' I snapped irritably, 'a bloody brain surgeon?'

Of course, he wasn't – he was the runner for Endemol, the TV production company responsible for such gems as *Can Fat Teens Hunt?*; and to confirm that I was in a purgatorial transit, he and his little colleague in the middle seat spent the rest of the flight yakking nonsense, while slurping kiddie drinks – vodka and lemonade, the alcopops of a criminally extended teenage. However, in a way they did me a favour, because they forced me to contemplate: first my own weird hypocrisy – here was I, a fearless psychogeographer, ever-determined to assault the conventions of mass-transit systems, yet still falling prey to the most blinkered of herd instincts – and then, latterly, the view from the window.

It was a night flight, but even by day viewing the British Isles from the air can be a problematic endeavour: they're too damn small, and more often than not covered in cloud, like an ancient dessert submerged in whipped cream that's going off. At least, that's what I like to tell myself. When I grope back through the frayed card index of my memory, I do come across startling prospects I've experienced from the air: the west of Ireland, spread out below, a green counterpane bejewelled with tiny lochs; the snow-bound Orkney Islands, streaked black and white like killer whales in the hammered lead of the Pentland Firth.

But what marks these sights out is their singularity – they are not what you expect of Britain, and especially England – its unmade bed of a landscape, clut-

AIR TRAVEL - SEATING ARRANGEMENTS Ralph Steadman

tered with human leftovers. Moreover, they are views I experienced when I – if not the world – was still young. Still, there I was, and rather than listen to the he-wank, she-wank talk of my travelling companions, I decided to garner what I could from the darkling empyrean, the bejewelled cities of the plain – like inversions of the Milky Way – and the metropolises along our route: Birmingham, Manchester, then Glasgow itself, which seemed like transparent jellyfish, sparking with unknowable sentience.

What is it about flying? Why is it that what must, by any reasonable estimation, be the most exciting and extreme, technologically mediated experience any of us are ever likely to have – apart, that is, from radical surgery – is hedged round with such ineffable tedium vitae? Getting into a titanium tube? Being hurled by vast jet engines six miles high, then coasting down a cloudy slalom into another time zone? Why not squabble over the aisle seat, bore through Grisham wood pulp, goggle at the minikins cavorting on the seat back, or plug your ears with soft rock – do anything, in short, to avoid being fully conscious of this revolutionary, quintessentially Modernist experience: the 600 mph, hundreds of miles wide vantage of a superhero – or a god.

My hunch is that the way in which every aspect of air travel is trammelled by the ineffably dull – tedious airport architecture, monotonous muzak, anodyne announcements, superfluous consumer opportunities – is the result of an unconscious collective denial. After all, if flight crew wore winged helmets, and the Ride of the Valkyries came blasting over the PA as the plane picked up speed on the runway, then, when the oily behemoth slipped the surly bonds of gravity, the captain cried: 'Weeeee!', the latent anxieties of every passenger would be unleashed. Even if we survived the flight, we'd probably land determined never to do it again: 'Flying? What a trip! Once is enough for me.' And the whole go-round of work-consume-travel-die would grind to a halt.

As it is, plane flight is the most intense juxtaposition of the banal and the sublime available to humanity: we sit, belted in, eating dry-roasted peanuts, and veering between contemplating our own unavoidable mortality, and the bad karma of the person sitting next to us: it's bad enough to be working on *Can Fat Teens Hunt?*, but to *die* working on it, that, like, sucks. We sit, cramped (and in my case, thanks to the teeny-rotters, with my knees pressed into my eye sockets), while just beyond two layers of Plexiglas the very curvature of the earth can be glimpsed, squiggled across it the route map of St Brendan.

It's all enough to make anyone philosophic – except, that is, a bloody brain surgeon.

# Top 5 Winter Walks

Yes, it's that time of the year again, when the *Independent* magazine's panel of experts: radio presenter, Libby Purves; comedy terrorist, Aaron Barschak; Ban Ki-Moon, the UN Secretary-General; and me, meet together at a London hotel reeking of commercial sex and stale flatulence, to compile our list of the best brumal promenades. As with all such exercises, the aim is to achieve consensus – so these may not be the top walks, per se, but rather: the ones we can reasonably concur on. In no particular order, then:

*Walk 1: Herat to Kabul. Distance: approximately 400 miles. Conditions: fair to middling. Ability level: beginner.*

It's best to undertake this walk in mid-winter, as in summer temperatures soar. Make sure you have good boots but native clothing, as fancy gear may be ripped off your back by angry and impoverished tribesmen. At least one local dialect – Dari, Pashtun – is essential if you want to avoid being shot by resurgent Taliban, or abducted by hostile warlords. Army training – preferably Special Forces – is advisable, as is an unusual level of mental resilience and physical toughness. Antibiotics may be required.

I took this walk in the company of Rory Stewart, whose *The Places in Between* is a masterful account of his trek across Afghanistan in 2002, six weeks after the Taliban had fled. Stewart's account is so vivid that I was convinced I was pacing alongside him, rather than lying in bed, in south London, five years after the event, eating Christmas cake: slice after hunk, until the sheets were a treacherous morass of sticky crumbs.

*Walk 2: Netherton to Motherwell town centre. Distance: 6 miles. Conditions: poor. Ability level: advanced.*

It's a tough customer indeed who embarks on a walk along the Clyde Walkway, in the heart of the Scots Rust Belt, at this – or indeed any – time of year. It's wet, it's cold, and there are usually enormous shifting dunes of broken Buckfast Tonic wine bottles to negotiate. Local guides may be required – and interpreters.

I did the walk twice this Christmas; first by night, by the light of a Ban Ki-Moon, then by day, with Libby Purves. The Secretary-General was completely 'weirded out' by the overgrown graveyard at the foot of Dalzell Park, and found the Barons Haugh nature reserve equally intimidating. Purves, by contrast, took to the Clyde like a duck to water – in fact, this is no metaphor, for the award-winning radio presenter did indeed strip off then plunge into the Nambarrie tea-coloured river, which was in full spate. She swam downstream to the Strathclyde Country Park, before popping out again like a pink seal. I was impressed.

*Walk 3: Seething Lane to Westminster Palace via the Change, then back again via the Sun Inn. Distance: 4 miles. Conditions: 15 January 1665. Ability level: seeking preferment.*

Up and walked to Whitehall, it being still a brave frost and I in perfect good health, blessed be God. Met with Tanger committee, where I was accosted and most highly complimented by Lord Bellasses our new Governor, beyond my expectation or measure I could imagine he would have given any man. This I am well pleased with and may make good use of it. Then to the Sun, and finding Mistress Purves there away elle and I to a private cabinet where elle and I have été before; and there I had her company toute l'après-diner and had mon plein plaisir of elle. So home, and found there my wife and Mr Barschak, both got up as Moors. Mr Barschak and my lad, Tom, did then play upon their instruments most prettily until gone three a-clock. Supper and to bed.

*Walk 4: Lofthouse to The Sportsman's Arms Hotel at Wath. Distance: 7 miles. Conditions: grim up north. Ability level: Janet.*

A good sodden tramp on the North York Moors is more or less mandatory for anyone who wishes to consider themselves a heroic modern Briton in the Gordon Brown mode. Indeed, without us undertaking such walks it's hard to see democracy surviving. Look at Kenya and Pakistan – thousands of barefooted rioters, looting local branches of Cotswolds Outdoors for Meindl walking boots. I said as much to Ban Ki-Moon as we plodded across Dallowgill Moor, the rain driving into our faces, and he concurred: 'Without robust institutions, transparent election monitoring, and a generous supply of Kendall Mint Cake, it is hard to envision a –', before I shut him up by stuffing a glove in his mouth.

*Walk 5: Back to work. Distance: illimitable. Conditions: 7.5 per cent APR. Ability level: nearly superannuated.*

# RosaFullsizeFuckstick

. . . You take my impotence for example. Up until a few years ago the old todger was as big as a bloody battering ram: I used to *fear* my erections. Since then, well, I blame Nigerian traffic wardens. They come over here, can't speak the lingo and strut about the place slapping tickets on anything that moves – it's intimidating. I was coming out of the Cross Keys in Wilmslow and there was one of the bastards skulking under the moot hall having plastered a big yellow sticky one right across the Range Rover's windscreen. Well, I went to have it out with the blackguard – I wasn't about to be intimidated! I fought in eight world wars and put down the bloody Mau-Mau, man, armed only with a Martini-Henry! Anyway, to begin with he's cringing and scraping, but then he pulls some ghastly little fetish out of his tunic. Looks like a cat's paw wrapped in a hairball all tied round with kidney stones – fair gave me the willies, ha! if you'll forgive the pun – or rather, anti-pun – because it didn't give me the willies, it took mine away! Ever since I gave that illegal immigrant chappie a rollicking I haven't even caught sight of poor John Thomas, seems he's completely hidden away inside me. Saw the same thing in Malaya during the Emergency in the fifties, native wallahs would get the damn-fool idea their meat 'n' veg were sort of retreatin' inside their bodies – *lattah* they call it – thing is, in their case it was a bloody fantasy, in mine it's a reality. My missus, well, she may be getting on but she has certain perfectly reasonable expectations: a Tory government, no one frightening the horses, no redevelopment in Hungerford High Street, Sunday afternoon rumpy-pumpy right after matins – you get the photo. When I realised I wouldn't be able to service the old mare I got pretty antsy, I can tell you. Went to see the quack sharpish. Well, she's only some junior harridan sporting a Harriet Harman horror mask, ain't she. Has the bloody nerve to tell me I ought to be cutting out the sleepy Ribena and the fags at my age. My age! I explored the Lost-bloody-World and climbed the Empire State Building with my

I LOOK AT IT THIS WAY-SURE, THERE'S DISAPPOINTMENTS IN LIFE — YOU JUST HAVE TO GET OFF YER BACKSIDE AND DEAL WITH IT.

mitts up Fay Wray's jacksie so the likes of her could have free school milk. The chit wouldn't even write me a prescription for Viagra, told me it was 'contra-indicated' for a man of my age. That wasn't going to stop me, oh no. Jimmie Wemyss, mine host at the Bald Eagle in Netheridge, told me about this interweb thing, and how a chap can get anything he needs with a push of a button, so I ordered the contraption from little Freddie Dixon, and when it pitched up, he came up and got me started. Turns out you don't even need to go looking for the stuff, there are all sorts of obliging fellows out there who send jolly emails offering Viagra, Cialis, and even this sleepy Ribena in pill form called Ambien. But before I could even divvy up the old Diners' Club I got rather sucked into correspondence with them. I mean, I'm not *lonely* or anything, but the trouble and strife spends an awful amount of time with her committee work, and early February . . . well, the time before opening can lay heavy on a chap's hands. Besides, when you get a tinkle out of the blue yonder headed FuckStickAmpleFloyd, or GargantuanPenisBeau, well, it's a tonic in itself. I began writing back to Karen Knutsin, Stanislaw Baczmonski, Kumar Senthil, and all the other obliging souls out there in hyperworld. Nothing too personal, just stuff about the village, who's breaching planning regs with his fucking dreadful conservatory, and who's dipping his sheep in liquid MDMA then rogering 'em – harmless gossip, really.

Back they come – my emails – with more exciting headings: BodyPartEnlarged-Shawn and BarneySchlongBroad, well, I mean, who are they when they're at home! If they ever *are* at home. I imagine they're 'hanging out' on some Thai beach or other, with a whole tribe of itty-bitty little fillies to satisfy their every urge. Natural Manhood Enhancement, Watch it bigger day by day! – that's what they were offering me, but I preferred to keep 'em at arm's length. I said to Giles Woode at the Cock and Bull in Bent Parva: Y'know, I'm almost grateful to that bloody Nigerian for opening up a whole new realm of experience for me – it's something you don't expect at my age. Turns out Giles is no stranger to PenisPlumpingCarla himself. I'd no idea that – to coin a phrase – he needed 'easily to get male package'. Always assumed he'd lost it altogether during the Suez Crisis. Ho-hum, another bottle of Ribena, or are you riding?

# Bill Gates

You could've knocked me down with a semi-transparent pop-up ident of a feather when I got an email from Bill Gates. To begin with I thought the scrambled syntax, banjaxed grammar, and dubious content was yet another spammer: 'C'mon Big Boy see my lake glistens 4 U. All Xs pays bi me if U cum kwik.' But later I was called by an assistant who informed me that the multi-billionaire software tycoon wasn't trying to sell me Viagra, but rather wanted me and Ralph to join him at his $97m lakeside eco-mansion for what Gates terms a 'Think Week'.

'It'll be blue sky stuff,' the MicroWonk said. 'How you and Ralph view the future of space – and time – that kinda thing.'

'I'll tell you that for nothing,' I snapped. 'Time will go on, space will get bigger.'

'That's great, just great,' the WindowsWimp was not to be dissuaded. 'First-class tickets to Seattle will be delivered by courier later today.'

'But what if I don't want to come?' I became querulous.

'Try Viagra,' the MiniMonopolist said and hung up on me.

The trouble was that Ralph adores a freebie of this kind, and even though he was just back from Davos, where he'd been advising the head of the World Bank on corporate re-imaging, he insisted on going. Well, I couldn't let him set out alone, Ralph may be brilliant at taking a line for a walk, but off the page he lacks basic orientation skills.

Arriving at the serried concrete bobbins of Sea-Tac Airport on a brilliant winter's morning I couldn't face climbing into a cab. Instead, I put Ralph in one and told him to break the ice over at Bill's place, while I stretched my legs. 'For Christ's sake, Will,' Ralph bridled, 'what am I going to talk to him about?'

'You both dig Da Vinci – ask to see his Leonardo stuff. He has the Codex Leicester, cast your eye over it, then get out your pen and begin flicking ink – I'm sure he'll see the funny side.'

I slogged through the suburb of McMicken Heights and Crystal Springs Park, down to the deliriously named Interurban Avenue. Picking up the Green River Trail I trod on beside the rows of poplars screening off the Boeing Plant. The Pacific North-west always invigorates me, with its soft, temperate climate and its boundless woodiness – all those trees, photosynthesising like Billy-o; it's a tonic to the air sacs.

The long tramp into town on Fourth Avenue would've been dull, but I had work to do. Bill had set up a SharePoint website for the three of us, where we could post sketches, notes, and supplementary information relating to the space/time Think Week. I had my Tablet PC with me, so using invaluable OneNote and OneWord software I was able to post stuff as I went; such as musings on Bill's brilliant coinage 'Creative Capitalism', and how it might possibly relate to the man walking ahead of me, pushing a supermarket cart piled with old tin cans and festooned with plastic bags, who couldn't seem to keep his pants up.

Past the Quest Field and on into downtown; darkness was falling, and if it hadn't been for the unearthly up-light of the computer screen, making of me an ambulatory ghoul, I'm sure some of the shambling homeless might've clubbed together to mug me. As it was, I took Madison Street to Washington Park, then the long scuzzy tongue of the Evergreen Point Floating Bridge across Lake Washington to the lakeside community of Medina.

It had been a twenty-five-mile walk, and it was now past midnight. I was cold, hungry, and thought the very least I could expect from a man with a net personal worth of $56 billion was a cheese toastie and a cup of tea – but not a bit of it. The familiar goofy boy scout's visage peered through the security louvers, then Gates admitted me to a nerdish bedlam: piles of old Marvel comics and empty Yakult cartons were scattered everywhere, an Atari games console was pinging in the sink. Ralph was in the conversation pit, making paper darts out of pages from the Codex, and I don't think he can possibly object if I tell you, gentle reader, that he was a little tipsy.

'You tossers!' I cried. 'While you've been behaving like overgrown teenagers, I've been sorting out the whole space-time continuum.'

'Gee,' Bill said, 'I'm sorry – I guess. Melinda's vacationing at the moment, and I kinda let things go. Please tell me your thoughts – I'm sure they're real inneresting.'

'The shift key – get rid of it!'

'But why?'

'So no one will ever again, anywhere in the world, be able to conceive of typing the words "SharePoint" or "OneNote".'

'Or SpaceTime!' Ralph bellowed from the pit.

# Before the Law

Feeling like the protagonist of Kafka's fragment 'Before the Law', I cycled across town on a windy February evening to the Royal Courts of Justice. They're Gothic, certainly, but the Gothic is so entrenched in British architecture – as style, recursive style, fakery and mockery – that to call the Courts this is a mere allusion. They are bulbous complacent stupid Gothic, Gothic as an elaboration on High Victorian delusions of mightiness and rightiness, with finials of lumpy complacency buttressed by hefty hypocrisy. It's no surprise to discover that George Edward Street, the criminal architect responsible for designing them, originally qualified as a solicitor.

Who but a solicitor would conceive of decorating the gates of the Law with the carved heads of celebrated judges and lawyers? Who but a solicitor would have the plodding nerve to surmount them with Jesus, Moses and Solomon, while the poor litigants are immortalised as a fighting dog and cat. And who but the Ministry of Justice – crazy Kafkaesque name, crazy Kafkaesque institution – would dream of hiring out the Great Hall by the hour, so that City types can trough down in splendour, and applaud their own huge feats of avarice, and tiny ones of beneficence.

I was here almost a year ago, called upon by a charity called War Child. Having been offered the opportunity to fundraise at a bond traders' dinner, they were desperate for a speaker and asked me to step into the breach. On that occasion things went reasonably well – if begging is ever OK. I doffed my rhetorical cap, and the rich guys listened respectfully to my spiel, before tossing a 10p coin into it. In fact, they divvied up a couple of hundred grand, but proportionally – given there were trillions in the Great Hall – I was a *Big Issue* seller in a suit.

This year War Child came knocking again, and I didn't have the gall to give them knock-back. True, I do believe in the work they're doing – helping kids in war zones, feeding them, clothing them, building them schools – it's just I'm not

BLOTS
ON ANY
LANDSCAPE

Ralph STEADman 2008

sure it's them that should be doing it. Charities and other NGOs follow in the wake of our government's foreign adventuring like vultures with sociology degrees, feeding off the carrion left behind on the battlefield. They alight for a few months or years, putting out celebrity-endorsed pop CDs back home to fund their endeavours, and then flap away again to feed on more Humanism.

Still, any good is better than no good, and so it was that I found myself, within the gates of the Law, watching the black ties getting spattered with red wine, and admiring the multicoloured up-lights playing upon the pillars of the great hall. It transpired that this lot were different: not as grand as last year's CEOs, these poor cousins were responsible for leveraged finance and syndicated loans. Hmm, and the dread credit crunch was squeezing them until the Faberge pips popped out. Why, some of them would only be getting six-figure bonuses this year. Nevertheless, the dinner was an opportunity for these nabobs of debt creation to give themselves glitzy awards with snappy names like 'Best Arranger of Project Finance Loans', and 'Best Arranger of Turkish Loans'.

Now, I like to come into an environment and try to understand it, even one as bizarrely unwholesome as this. So, I dutifully asked the studious young man seated next to me what exactly a 'mezzanine loan' was, and he explained that it was a loan where the borrowers' failure to repay would result in the loaners acquiring equity in their business. Simple, really: banking as a kind of invasion of the body snatchers.

On they went, to the grossly amplified strains of pop hits, sashaying up to the lectern and booming out such rousing speeches as 'We did the Imperial Tobacco loan!' It felt like aeons – yet it was only an hour or so. Finally, it was my turn to approach the gatekeeper of the Law. I spoke for twenty minutes or so, giving a run-down on War Child's work, exhorting the assembled extremely wealthy people to divvy up for building toilets and schools in Iraq, and retraining traumatised child soldiers in the Congo, before ending up with a description of one case history: a twelve-year-old Afghani girl raped by her uncle and then imprisoned for – you guessed it – adultery.

It was then that I began to hear a distinct susurration spreading through the Great Hall and lapping against the pretentious pillars: they were talking. And not just one or two of them, exchanging the odd remark – but entire tables chatting away while they slugged back the Rioja. I stopped, and boomed at them over the PA: 'I'm wondering what exactly it is that you're discussing that can possibly be more important than a child being raped?' But it was a stupid question, because I knew already: it was money – and there was a certain justice in that, oh yes.

# Peter Grimy

To Sadler's Wells to see Opera North's production of Britten's *Peter Grimes*. I'm not that familiar with the piece – or at least, I didn't think I was – but it turned out that I had absorbed it in some occult way: the shingle of Suffolk beaches pounding the libretto into my psyche, the winds over the marshes blowing haunting skirls into my inner ear. Which is just as well, because the boiler had been on the fritz for the past few days, and the unaccustomed warmth of that many London bourgeois gathered together sent me into a deep swoon.

A spare setting: tawny stage, umber backdrop; the naked corpse of a well-built man lying in the mid-distance; instruments mimicking the cry of gulls. Is this not my fundamental state of mind – in dream or awake? As for the tormented, abusive relationships between fathers and their putative sons – is this not the very stuff of my life? The only thing that jibes is the small-minded Aldeburgh burghers themselves.

Britten based the opera on George Crabbe's 'The Borough', and said that this minute dissection of small town mores spoke to him, saying 'the more vicious the society, the more vicious the individual'. In Crabbe's original poem,

> He wish'd for one to trouble and control;
> He wanted some obedient boy to stand
> And bear the blow of his outrageous hand;
> And hoped to find in some propitious hour
> A feeling creature subject to his power.

Some assert that Montagu Slater's original libretto made the relationship between the fisherman, Grimes, and his two apprentices explicitly pederastic, and that Britten and his partner, Peter Pears, toned it down. I say, if you want a gay opera you call it *The Magic Flute*. But this is by the by, for by the time the lights went down – and then up again – I was a Grimes convert.

GRIM RETURNS

And resolved to entrain the very next day for Aldeburgh itself. The town has always had an ambivalent relationship with its famous composing son. Some say that Britten kept himself aloof – others that he was shunned. Just as some say *Peter Grimes* is an essential part of the operatic canon – while others deride it as 'Gilbert and Sullivan without the tunes'. Whatever the truth of either assertion, this shingle strand with its row of austere, high-gabled houses, and its jewel box of a moot hall, has an end-of-the-world feel.

But I'm getting ahead of myself: on the way up, the train stopped at Ipswich, and my carriage pulled alongside a singular man. He was young – no more than thirty – and morbidly obese. He was sitting on a specially reinforced electric buggy, talking on a mobile phone. Somewhat inappropriately, he wore a tracksuit, while a novelty bumper sticker on the front of his buggy read: 'IF YOU DON'T LIKE MY DRIVING CALL 0800 F**CK OFF'. I found this a disturbing – and threatening – sight, and wondered whether he was some latter-day Grimes, waiting for a new apprentice to clout.

My long-time editor, Liz Calder, who has moved to the locale, drove me into Aldeburgh and we went for a walk on the beach. I wanted to see Maggi Hambling's *Seashell* sculpture, which has attracted so much opprobrium from the locals. A memorial to Britten, the rim of the shell is pierced with a line from *Peter Grimes*: 'I hear those voices that will not be drowned.' Some say the paint that's been slung across its shiny concavities and steely ribbing is a homophobic assault on the dead composer; others that it's merely local yobs. One thing's for sure, the Aldeburgh rite, whereby the inhabitants of the borough stomp up and down the beach, to and from Thorpeness, is as highly ritualised as any Neapolitan promenade. Moreover, there can be nothing more frightening on the Suffolk coast than encountering a man in a Barbour, armed with one of those extended arms used to hurl balls for retrievers to . . . um, retrieve.

In the final act of the opera, Peter Grimes, having done for a second apprentice, is ordered out to sea by an old fishermen. He is to go so far that he can no longer see the little moot hall and then scuttle the boat. Standing in the gathering dusk, the cold wind whipping in off the North Sea, and the lights of the nuclear power station at Sizewell, five miles up the coast, beginning to twinkle, it suddenly seemed like a good idea to emulate this. So I stripped off, and leaving Liz safely wedged in the Hambling, I struck out for the horizon with my famously languid butterfly stroke . . .

And came to, back in the stalls at Sadler's Wells. Yes, dear reader, it was a dream; except, that is, for the obese man in the tracksuit – no one could make that up.

# Heart of Lightness

I entrained at London Bridge, my fingers gummy with the residue of an almond Danish, and hungry as ever for the flatlands of the Thames estuary. This interzone was where my mission began in the late 1980s: to untangle human and physical geography. I've never wavered from my conviction that there's something bizarre about all those millions of Londoners who have never seen – or even seen represented – the point where the River Thames flows into the North Sea. That there can be a location so near by and yet so under-imagined – that alone tells us that the world remains strange to us.

Conrad's *Heart of Darkness* takes its readers on a hellish voyage up 'a mighty big river . . . resembling an immense snake uncoiled . . . its tail lost in the depths of the land', but it begins opposite Gravesend in Kent, as Marlowe and his transfixed listeners wait on the *Nellie*, a cruising yawl, for the ebbing tide. The conceit is nice: the most famous tale of the dark heart of Africa is told in a place that, while well comprehended in Conrad's day, has since become a curiously blank spot on the mental map.

Not that you'd be wise to say this to the people of Gravesend, who presumably know full well where they are: pottering up and down the Regency terraces and occasionally glancing across the ecru river to the container port of Tilbury on the far shore. I had time to kill: I'd missed Antony at London Bridge, and he'd then missed his stop and gone on to the Medway. We oriented ourselves with mobile phones, echo-locating bats with the faces of middle-aged men, flapping around an estuarine cave. We met eventually in the covered market. Digital watches and AAA batteries, Scottie's Liver Treats and Doggie Chews – all of it being sold from under the bulging eyes of a Queen Victoria who's made – Antony established by tapping her breast – from terracotta.

Maglorian, the Jack Russell puppy, led us out of town between metal-bashing

LEAST EXPECTED

sheds and the redoubts of the old batteries, while Antony talked to someone on the phone about a plan to climb Mont Blanc. His energy was preposterous: his latest show had opened the previous evening at the White Cube in town, its centrepiece, *Firmament*, a single 'expanded field' constructed from 1,770 steel elements and 1,019 steel balls. The catalogue described it as: 'an assembled matrix of volumes that map a celestial constellation while also implying the form of a body'.

To me it looked like a big steel girder bloke fighting to escape the gallery.

The river embankment skirted Eastcourt, Shorne and Higham marshes – we dutifully plodded on. Ahead we could see the burn-offs of the oil refinery at Canvey Island flaring in the dullness. Why – it bothered me – is this place so overlooked? Certainly there are plastic shells on the shore – but there are also oyster catchers dibbing in the mud. Besides, this is one of the most celebrated literary landscapes in England: the Cliffe marshes, where the young Pip is discovered by Magwitch at the beginning of *Great Expectations*.

Now, at the fort where the escaped convict took refuge, there's a small flotilla of dinghies drawn up on the bank of a flooded gravel pit, and a two-kilometre-long conveyor belt was rattling aggregate across the land to a cement works. Instead of a prison hulk, there was a huge Chinese freighter beating downstream, the containers stacked on its deck presumably jam-packed with dormant VDUs, PCs and plastic pianos, all headed for Shanghai, to be reawakened and played upon. Conrad's novel was an early assault upon the relentless logic of globalisation: his Kurtz would have understood only too well the silent horror of this ghostly ship loaded with detritus.

On we plodded and came upon Redham Marsh, a demented Teletubby landscape of green hummocks and greener dells: the deathly playground of Second World War anti-aircraft batteries. Travellers' ponies cropped the sward in between long rows of identical reinforced concrete ammunition stores. I explained to Antony that the individual Hepatitis C virus was an icosahedron-shaped blob only fifty millimetres across – so small that it cannot reflect visible light, and so is technically colourless. It seemed the right thing to say here in the whispering, once-malarial marsh.

We turned inland for Cliffe, Pip's native village. The puppy trotted at my heels: a tiny dog on a great plain. We were heading back towards the city now: 'The water shone pacifically; the sky, without a speck, was a benign immensity of unstained light; the very mist on the Essex marsh was like a gauzy and radiant fabric, hung from the wooded rises inland, and draping the low shores in diaphanous folds. Only the gloom to the west, brooding over the upper reaches, became more sombre every minute, as if angered by the approaching sun.'

# The Great
# Vomit Wave of '08

Don't read this over breakfast!

Who knows how it all began? A householder, rising from stool somewhere in the American Midwest – a resident of this 'ville or that 'berg, a regular blue-collar Joe who's just that little bit over-extended; he rises from making void of his natural waste products, and that's the better part of him gone, swirling in the bowl. He, his life, his wife, their kids, the sweat of their brows, it's all been off the back of a loan that's been bought and sold and traded – locked up in an impenetrable black box, given a triple A credit rating and punted from one side of the globe to the other. Our guy, he understands that it's all about to be flushed down the pan: he looks out the window and there's a car idling by the kerb with two thick-necked gum-chewers in the front seats: the repo men. His gorge rises, he's gripped by unspeakable nausea.

That's one scenario, or perhaps the Great Vomit Wave of '08 began somewhere else altogether. In Paris, where a heretofore undistinguished bond trader for the Banc de France, feeling a little dyspeptic, and aware that his trading account was considerably in the red, climbed out on to the waste pipes of the Pompidou Centre after a particularly large and fishy lunch. The *prix*, he realised, was no longer *fixe*. Looking down at the *salade mixte* of wannabe mime artists, the phalanxes of marauding Benelux au pair girls, the West Africans who had swum the Mediterranean to sell glass beads to the natives of the *16me arrondissement*, he may well have been gripped by the urge to let fly with a great red, white and blue-briny torrent.

Top down, or bottom up, the Great Vomit Wave of '08 was under way. Suggestible creatures, humans, and there's nothing more likely to make them feel sick than someone being sick in the vicinity. The repo men, feeling the yawning pit of their own personal debt, reeled down the windows of their Grand Cherokee and hurled without reservation. The streams merged into a rivulet of sick that snaked along the suburban street. Desperate housewives emerged on to their front stoops, and catching that distinctive acid odour, lost control of their own consumerism; they coughed, they heaved, they brought forth more and more vomit that cascaded down the Carpenter Gothic stairs to join the rivulet; and so it became a river – and then a torrent.

In Paris the hefty plash of the bond trader's spew hit lovers and existentialists without regard for their finer feelings. Liberty, equality, fraternity! What conceivable use could there be for these lofty ideals when puke was all over the *place*? But worse, far worse was to come: while the Great Vomit Wave gathered in amplitude and came crashing along the Grands Boulevards, back in the States the news crews were aloft, the blades of their choppers whipping the colloidal barf into a vortex of Ps and Qs. In the local mall the teenagers looted LL Bean for swimsuits and Bermudas. While actually hurling themselves, they smashed the windows of the surf shop, took the boards, and soon were hanging ten on the very curling peak of the wave. Surfing in the Midwest! It could only ever happen during such a cataclysm.

The news crews transmitted the terrifying pictures of the barf boar to their stations, and the stations packaged them to the networks, and the networks broadcast them to the world. O! Foolish Humanity! O! Lackaday! When will you melt down the false idol of globalisation! When will you learn to pay attention first and foremost to what's on the end of your own fork! Those sickening images of sick – they, too, were a wave of nausea that coursed around the earth. A Japanese salary

man surfing on his 3G phone; a Brazilian truck driver stopping for a beer at a wayside café, a Kikuyu tribesman lingering outside the window of a TV shop – they all saw the awful images of the Great Vomit Wave, they all felt the spasms, they all coughed the cough, they all smelt the dread regurgitation of all that they had once ingested.

What is this thing called Man, who eats so many things? Who requires so many services – pampering, petting, smooching and smooching – simply to *keep it all down*? For that was the worst thing about the Great Vomit Wave of '08; in the West and the rest of the affluent world, the people threw up stuff they hadn't even particularly wanted in the first place: they felt the searing pain as the corners of electrical goods scraped their gullets; but elsewhere, the poor people dry-heaved, for, although racked by nausea, they had nothing to void.

Central Bankers hastily assembled to discuss the liquidity crisis, and found themselves knee-deep in each other's puke. It was all getting out of hand: parts of Bangladesh, Micronesia and the Netherlands were already undervomit. If there weren't drastic action soon, civilisation would come to an end, not with a bang but H'-h'-h'-heuuurrrregggh! The Prime Minister convened Cobra in the bunker beneath Number Ten Downing Street. All traces of the indecision that had marred the first months of his premiership had vanished: this was a big, tough man – a leader, with his gaze fixed on the verdict of history. 'Gentlemen,' he said to the police chiefs and army generals, the spooks and the medics. 'We must find a way to stop the people puking, but first –' He clapped his hand across his mouth, leapt up, and dashed from the room, the first among a myriad who felt equally nauseous.

# I Rendezvoused with Thanet

To Broadstairs, not to bathe, it being April, but merely to take the air. The Isle of Thanet has always been a little problematic for me; I can't even say it without recalling Ian Dury's lines: 'I rendezvoused with Janet / Quite near the Isle of Thanet / She looked just like a gannet. . .' etc. Somehow the great bard of the Kilburn High Road perfectly summed up this, the very coccyx of Britain, with its seafowl and its foul maidens.

Of course, seldom has anywhere more gentrified become more chavvy. Dickens, an habitué of the town, has one of his characters in *The Pickwick Papers* almost expire with relief once she reaches the haven of the Albion Hotel in Broadstairs, having had to endure the day-tripping of Margate en route. Dickens wrote to a friend of the town, that '[It] was and is, and to the best of my belief will always be, the chosen resort and retreat of jaded intellectuals and exhausted nature; being, as this Deponent further saith it is, far removed from the sights and noises of the busy world, and filled with the delicious murmur and repose of the broad ocean.'

He eventually bought the misnamed Bleak House, that still stands above the little horseshoe bay, looking not remotely grim, but more like a castellated Victorian fantasia on chivalric domesticity. What, I wonder, would he make of the town now, perfused as it is with tracksuited, gell-haired denizens of Margate and Ramsgate? Indeed, the whole of this coast feels like some suburb of outer east London, so full is it of the sights and noises of the busy world.

The sandy bay which is the town's focus remains, girded by white cliffs of chalk and terraced houses, complete with micro-inter-war pleasure gardens and a lift down to the beach that looks like an off-whitewashed crematorium chimney. There's Morrelli's, the beautifully preserved 1950s gelateria, where you can get Jammy Dodgers sundaes, and glass mugs of vaguely caffeinated froth, then consume them under a bizarre oil painting of a flooded Venice – the water creeping up

METAL DETECTORS AT DAWN 'Thanet be light!'

Ralph STEADman 2008

over St Mark's. These are good things, and up the steep High Street there are chip shops and charity shops and Doyle's Psychic Emporium ('Open Your Mind'), and a sweet shop selling orange crystals, spearmint pips and liquorice wheels. There's even an optician's called See Well.

We hung out on the beach, fetching teas from the Chill Time café. One ageing hopeful came metal-detecting along the strand, Dr Who gadget held out in front of him, nuzzling the sand. Then another came up along, his gaze fixed on the gritty mother lode, his headphones clamped over his cartilaginous ears. Disaster! One metal detector detected the other, and one treasure seeker grabbed for the other's wand. A vicious mêlée ensued as the two men fought for the right to possess these found objects. The kids and I sat in the beach hut and laughed like gannets.

A happy scene, but come nightfall and the profile tyres began to screech on the tarmac, and the darkness was full of harsher, more discordant cries. I took the dog for a walk in the local park. The blackout was complete, but I was aware of the presence of many others. In any large city these might have been furtive seekers after fleeting, anonymous congress, but here, in Broadstairs, they turned out to be enormous gaggles of teenagers, wheeling around on the mown grass, their mobile phones held under their chins so that the wan up-light weirdly illuminated their vestigial features. As I grew closer to one of these gaggles I became aware of an insistent and peculiar gobbling noise; the sound of many breaking voices intoning 'Fuck off, fuck off, fuck off,' over and over again.

I blame Hengist and Horsa for Broadstairs's current fall from gentility. The two Danes – or, possibly, Germans – were invited by King Vortigern of Kent to come here in the fifth century: an early form of economic migration. One thousand five hundred years later, in 1949, the anniversary of their arrival was commemorated by some latter-day pseudo-Vikings: Danish oarsmen who completed the voyage in a replica boat. They landed on the sands below Dickens's Bleak House, and the local municipality laid on a slap-up feed of hot soup, cold poultry and potatoes with fresh salad in ample portions. Later there was heavy-footed dancing to the accompaniment of Joseph Muscant's Salon Orchestra.

But not content with such a welcome the town councillors foolishly changed the name of Main Bay to Viking Bay. Doubtless they thought this would cement Anglo-Danish relations, but so far as I can see the main upshot has been that the town's inhabitants go berserk from time to time. Waiting for the train back to London, I overheard two Thanet warriors discoursing on the platform: ''E's a cunt inne,' said one, 'always bum-licking, but if you turns yer back on 'im 'e'll give you a smack in the mouf.' They were drinking Stella Artois, if only it were reassuringly expensive.

# Maglorian

To paraphrase Oscar, 'Some people come to resemble their pets, that is their tragedy; some people don't come to resemble their pets, that is theirs.' I think in this context of the German woman I have met twice now walking her Leonbergers down the road near Clapham Junction where the boys and I wait to get the bus on the way back from school. The woman is frowsty with a leonine head of pink, dyed hair, thick round the middle – she's only five foot two, or thereabouts and must weigh getting on for ten stone – and as for the dogs . . . well, they're not called Leonbergers for nothing, this the nearest thing you get to lion that's still canine. Their dotty owner – who snapped 'Leonberger!' at me, when I asked what breed they were (as if it were entirely obvious) – must have to go out with a shovel to pick their dung up.

How much more appealing is the equally dotty woman I've encountered by night in Battersea Park, her white perm flaring around her pretty face, her retroussé nose questing the night air. Around her ankles bounce five creatures that closely resemble Japanese Manga comic creatures, or vaguely canine Teletubbies. They are, it transpires, Bichon Frisées, and she loves them to bits. Loves them so much, that when she told me her husband had said he'd leave her if she got any more, I detected a distinct *froideur* in her tone. This is one fellow who may come home one night to discover that the dogs have eaten his dinner, his house, and half of his income for the foreseeable future.

I swore that I wouldn't become one of those dog owners who anthropomorphise their pets, and attribute to them all sorts of qualities they manifestly don't possess, the sort of Jilly Cooperesque twerp who puts up monuments to the animals who died in two world wars, incised with the words 'They Had No Choice'. Of course they had no fucking choice – and they had no say in your bloody memorial either. But then there's Maglorian, my Jack Russell, who isn't so much a dog as . . . a furry

DOG DAYS. Ralph Steadman 2008

baby. There was a piece in the *Daily Telegraph* a few weeks ago saying that people who sleep with their pets in the bed are laying themselves open to diseases, however, at the end it was conceded that you're far more likely to contract something nasty from your kids.

Same diff' Chez Self, where dogs, children, whatever – they all end up in the big duvet tent. No doubt much like the home life of our dear new London Mayor. Still, dogs have it over children in all sorts of other ways: they don't ask continuous – and impossible to answer – questions; in two words: they never grow up; and – better still – they *really* like going for walks.

But this being confessed, I have a ruthless streak when it comes to Maglorian. I had him up that vet to get his balls scythed off as soon as I could. I wanted him docile, I wanted him to be a homebody, I favoured the idea that he would become a superb counter-tenor barker, as against him shtupping every little waggle-tailed slapper in the neighbourhood. Also, it means that when he goes after balls in the park – which he does all the time, under the signal delusion that he can play football – it means I can quip: 'He wants your ball . . . because he hasn't got any of his own.'

Ah, park life. I thought I'd done it to death, I thought I'd covered the pondfront, what with working in parks for the Greater London Council in my twenties, followed by nearly two decades of having children under eight; how wrong I was, with Maglorian to be walked three times a day the intensity of my relationship with parks – and their habitués – has deepened inexorably. And where there are parks, there are other dog owners, which in our part of sarf London means owners of huge savage-looking dogs with studded collars, straining on the end of their leashes while some character with tattoos/gold teeth/gold bracelets/gold necklace/ sidearm (delete where appropriate) says, 'Back! Fang/Blood/Bruvver!' Also, delete where appropriate, and frankly, such is the ire that these playlets of male impotence masked by canine potency induce in me, that I'd happily put the Staffordshire Bull Terrier/Bullmastiff cross's owner to sleep.

Until, that is, you begin talking to the buggers, and they turn out to be perfectly mellow fellows, with nothing but sweet, cuddly, loveable things to say about their furry babies: 'Nah, nah, mate – 'e's not a fightin' dog, 'e's great wiv kids – blinding, really.' Blinding indeed, and bark-stripping as well, the trees in the local park look as if an incendiary bomb has been let off in the vicinity, a nice conceit, given that before the Blitz this open space was covered in terraces.

The only question is, is it the man who's taught the dog its parenting skills, or vice versa? Oscar would know.

# Clipping Ralph

A disturbing tale comes from Ralph in New York. I'm not sure we're going to be able to let him out on his own in future. Apparently in an antic state, he decided to take a party of friends over from Manhattan to Staten Island on the ferry. Being Ralph – and committed to the transgression of all norms – he wanted his party to dodge the ferry fare, assuming that since his first trip stateside, in 1970, it would've risen five-hundredfold, from a nickel to $25. Much to his chagrin, the ferry was entirely free, having been subsidised by Mayor Bloomberg, in a vote-grabbing move aimed at improving the Islanders' self-esteem.

Not without reason is Staten Island known as 'the forgotten borough', during the Second World War it was in fact occupied by the Japanese, without anyone in New York – or Washington – even noticing. The Imperial Army was there for so long, that many of its troops set aside their weapons and some laboured on the poultry and dairy farms that at that time still occupied the south of the island, while others took lucrative positions in advertising on Madison Avenue – but that's another story: Rising Sun: *The Imperial Japanese Army and Soap Powder* by Chaim Medvedev, Parallel Books, $24.95.

I digress. Having disembarked from the scandalously free ferry, Ralph went in search of a bar he remembered from four decades before. Outside the neoclassical nugget of the Staten Island Supreme Courthouse he accosted a gentleman known only – even to himself – as 'John'. 'John' was having a cigarette during a recess from a case he was involved in, in - he told Ralph – an 'advocacy role'. Ralph took this fellow in his sharp Italian suit, wraparound shades and a loud Versace tie, entirely at his word, and received directions to the Clipper Bar and Restaurant.

Ralph, the Rip Van Winkle *de nos jours*, was a little put out by the new construction on the island, when he was last there the old Art Deco buildings predominated – now it's the same old rectilinear, steel and glass boretasamagorica as anywhere else in the 'developed' world. Be that as it may, Ralph and his posse settled into the Clipper, and fell into conversation with a lively fellow called 'Bob', wearing a leather windcheater with a healthy bulge under its armpit.

'Bob' was much taken by Ralph's incessant scrawling on the American flag beer mats that were scattered along the bar, and as Ralph drew more, so 'Bob' fed him with mats, until they had quite a stack. Meanwhile, the business of the Clipper went on around them. Ralph had a hamburger, and a woman came in and barked: 'Two hamboigers, and d'ya have any relish?' Trying to be helpful Ralph reached for the ketchup and said, guilelessly, 'Is this relish?'

'Dat's not relish, shtoopid!' The woman snorted.

'Sorry,' Ralph said – being, at least by adoption, an English bourgeois. 'I didn't know.'

'Well, ya oughta!' she snapped back and that was when it all kicked off.

'Are you insulting the honour of Italian-Americans?' 'Bob' said, leaning threateningly over Ralph.

'Er, no,' Ralph replied. 'I mean, I've never given it much thought, but I suppose if they need a little insulting I'm the man for the job.'

'I should say you are.' 'Bob' plucked one of Ralph's customised beer mats from the bar. 'Look at this, in this toiny space you've succeeded in insulting Staten Island, desecrating the Stars and Stripes, and impugning the honour of all Italian-American women.'

'Impugning?'

'Yeah, impugning – what's wrong with that?'

'Nothing, it's just not an expression you expect to hear in the Clipper.'

'OK, I've had enough outta you!' And with that, 'Bob' pulled an evil-looking automatic from inside his jacket, and used the snub barrel to indicate that Ralph should leave. Needless to say, Ralph's free-ferry friends faded.

Outside the Clipper 'John' fell in with them, and the two Mafiosi – for that, Ralph realised, was what they were – marched him off along the Franklin Delano Roosevelt Boardwalk. Ralph essayed a few lame jests such as: 'What use was a board*walk* to FDR?' But by then it was clear that the enraged Staten Islanders weren't to be jollied from their dark mood.

Despite being on his way to being clipped, Ralph still managed to take in his surroundings, marvelling at the suburban – almost bosky – character of this, the largest of the five boroughs. It was only once they'd crossed Latourette Park and mounted the ominously named Todt Hill, that he thought he really ought to put up a fight: 'Listen, guys,' he said emolliently, 'believe me, my pictures have been

AMERICAN SUNSET ON

ATEN ISLAND BEER MAT Ralph STEADman 2008

known to insult anyone, regardless of nationality, creed, ethnicity or sexual orientation. Don't you think, as believers in America, land of opportunity, you should, ah, give some other groups a hand in my execution?'

This gave 'John' and 'Bob' pause for thought. They're probably still at it, but Ralph managed to sneak away and hide in the back of a garbage truck. Phew!

# Down and Out
# in Beverley Hills

Nobody much talks about the homeless in Los Angeles. My hunch is that there's a kind of collective denial: in this, the most illimitable – and yet curiously individuated – of megalopolises, the homeowners tend to assume that being without one can't be that bad; after all, the weather's always good – there's benches, and seventy-odd miles of white sand beach. The homeless – they can just hang out, then stroll the boulevards; while those who're saddled with the upkeep of mile after mile of Tudor revival, Spanish Mission, and Streamline Moderne, have to feel the acid burning through their duodenums, while the oil price hikes, and they sit, marooned, for hour after hour on the Harbour Freeway.

But it ain't true – this is a floor covering of a city, rolled out across a desert floor, and at night, the thermometer plummets. You see the results of this in the skin of the homeless, which is annealed by day then chilled by night, until their faces are as tanned as hides. In the darkness they huddle beneath the freeway overpasses, then when the sun rises, like lizards, they emerge to sop up the heat on the sidewalks.

I saw a lot of the homeless in Los Angeles – because I spent the entire week I was there on the streets, travelling at 3mph. I walked from LAX to downtown, via the Baldwin Hills, Crenshaw, West Adams and South Central. I walked from downtown to Hollywood, via Echo Park, Wilshire Boulevard, Fairfax and Melrose. I walked through Beverly Hills to Culver City, then back again. On Saturday – a rest day – I merely trolled across Hollywood, then headed up through Runyon Canyon Park to Mulholland Drive, then back down Laurel Canyon.

On the last, and longest day, I walked from Sunset Boulevard to Santa Monica, then along the coast to Venice, around Marina Del Ray, then past the Ballona Wetlands and back to the airport. It was my longest urban walking tour to date – especially given that there was a London leg from my house to Heathrow via Pinewood Studios as well – and I couldn't possibly do justice to the experience

WILL WALKS THE CITY OF DREAMS

236

in 8,000 words – let alone 800. You'll have to wait for the book: *Walking to Hollywood*, which – once it's written – will doubtless soon be a major motion picture, with Leonardo Di Caprio playing me (albeit with a body double for the walking sequences).

In the meantime, let me offer you this little teaser: on the final leg of the walk, leaving the humping marina behind, I set off along Lincoln Boulevard, past hoggish Harley Davidson dealerships, cut-price waxing salons, and young men twirling enormous cardboard arrows to advertise real estate. The sun squeezed my ear between its finger rays, and the exhaust of a thousand Escalades blatted into my face, while the paving slapped my soles. Then, horror of horrors, the sidewalk gave out, and I was in the middle of a dark wood of asphalt.

Luckily, a Virgil appeared to guide me through the auto-purgatory; to whit: John, who was fit and compact, with steel-grey hair, a yellow vest, khaki shorts and a leather rucksack. He'd been into Venice to do a little shopping, and now he was walking home. Yes, walking. 'I do it all the time,' he said as we moved along the verge at a brisk canter. 'The thing is, the pedestrian always has the right of way in California – the car drivers know that, so if they do hit you they drive off, because they'll be in big trouble.'

John lived in a house at the end of the bluff that rose up above the wetlands: 'I've been here twenty-seven years,' he told me, 'when I came this was a toxic swamp, but the developers who built Loyola Village over there had to clean it up as part of the deal. I think they've done a pretty good job.'

They had, the wetlands looked reassuringly wet: a green-and-blue jewel glittering in the mucky concrete of LA. Of course, Ballona has its own strange psychic currents: the discovery of ancient Native American burial sites is blamed by Angelenos for the hex that's been visited on various developers over the decades; among them Howard Hughes, who based his aircraft company here in the 1930s, constructing a two-mile-long airstrip (the longest in the world), and building the infamous *Spruce Goose*, a giant seaplane that only flew once, with Hughes himself at the controls.

John and I parted at the bluffs, where he took to a trail and I to the sidewalk – which had reappeared. At least, I think it was me who plodded on past motels and gas stations and golf courses to the airport. It might've been Leonardo Di Caprio – after all, he played Howard Hughes in Scorsese's *The Aviator*; but then, I suppose the stunts were a little more interesting than nearly being mowed down by traffic. And while Hughes may've become phobic about cutting his hair and fingernails, he wasn't truly homeless – he just looked like a dosser.

# Mad Masterchefs' Tea Party

The man with the cupcake stall in Northcote Road offered me one and when I tried to pay for it he said, 'No, no, it's the least I can do in return for your Psychogeography column.' This has to be about as good as it gets in the fan stakes: some writers have lust-crazed nymphets throwing themselves at them – I get a carob cupcake with very sweet icing. Still, I'm not knocking it, I know for a fact that Ralph has never received a gift of any kind from any of his myriad fans, and that when he reads about the cupcake he'll be demanding his share, but it's too late, mate, I wolfed the lot down on the spot, staring round me at the bourgeois mummies and daddies strolling from the specialist honey shop to the chichi French kids-wear shop.

In sarf London, the area round Northcote Road in Clapham is known as 'Nappy Valley', and there's something rather heartening about the way it lives up to its stereotype: there isn't anyone within the immediate vicinity who doesn't look either fully gravid, fully loaded, or both. Saving, possibly, the man who runs the cupcake stall, who next said, apropos of nothing that I could see: 'As Montaigne observed, to philosophise is to die.'

Now, this isn't what you expect of a cupcake-stall proprietor, although once I'd considered it, I was surprised that he didn't continue, because clearly he was glossing the old adage that man cannot live by bread alone, with the truth that neither may he become a metaphysical breatharian. Indeed, the more I thought about what the cupcake man said Montaigne said, the more I suspected that this was but a tiny slice of an exhaustive critique of the impact of globalisation on our patterns of consumption and our perception of the world, that the cupcake man had hidden in his stall.

I mean, that the likes of Jamie Oliver make a big noise about healthy eating for the lumpyproletariat while racking up fees advertising a supermarket chain certainly gets on my tits, but what it must do to Cupcake Man – who's manifestly involved in the honest labour of a culinary artisan – I hate to imagine. I see Cupcake Man, by night, working away on his treatise, his hands covered in icing burns, while on the TV in the corner of his garret (which is above the cupcake works), Oliver, Ramsay, Stein, Fearnley-Whittingstall, Blumenthal and all the rest of the celebrity egg-flippers are effing and blinding about a soufflé made from Eritrean goat's cheese.

And while we're thinking about Heston Blumenthal (crazy name, what persuaded his mum and dad to name him after some motorway services), he's recently invited me on one of his TV shows. Apparently, on these he recreates the cuisines of the past in order to 'tempt the jaded palates of the twenty-first century'. But there's nothing jaded about my palate at all, Heston, me old fat duck, I cleave to the notion that food is only shit waiting to happen, and that paying too much attention to what you shove in at one end is tantamount to coprophilia in advance.

No, give me an honest wedge of cheddar, a few oatcakes, a crisp apple and a carob cupcake and I'm a happy man. I once asked a gastronome friend of mine how far ahead he thought about the meals he would be having. He mused for a moment, before replying, 'Sometimes only a day or so, but mostly at least a week.' A week! Golly! Such foresight when it comes to an individual stomach is in marked contrast to the way humanity, like six billion locusts, is chomping through the planet's flora and fauna.

I'd like to organise a Masterchefs' tea party to be shown on all networks as part of the celebrations to mark the end of the Atlantic fisheries. We've only got a decade or so to go, so we'd better start planning it now. We'll need to speak to all the egg-flippers' agents and book 'em, we'll need to put all the relevant fish species on ice – so they're available, and we must secure the right venue; somewhere stupendous like the turbot hall . . . sorry, I mean 'turbine hall' . . . at Tate Modern.

I don't think any old punter should be allowed to eat the last cod, plaice, lobster or mackerel – it must be left to the finest palates we have to savour those final fishy riches for the rest of us; when they're done, they can simply move round a place and begin on the next endangered species. Montaigne had it wrong: to satirise is to die – a little, while these great chefs prove the truth of that toothsome adage: you are what you eat. Since they prepare – and eat – everything, it's they who are the world. Whereas the likes of me? Well, I'm just a sweet little cupcake, now aren't I?

# Hot Nuts

The sauna, or steam bath, has to be the most localised form of travel that we can engage in. Don't bother with jetting off to the diminishing equatorial rainforest because the summer weather here has been crap – simply march along to your local leisure centre, strip off in the utilitarian changing room, then immerse yourself in the microclimate. A properly maintained sauna has the same relative humidity as the Sahara or the Namib deserts; disregard the tiles that look as if they've been grouted with snot, the slatted benches greased with the essential oils of a thousand buttocks – narrow your dry eyes and the safety light, behind its wire mesh, will mutate into the hurting disc of the sun. If you keep the temperature well jacked-up and make sure to souse those rocks with plenty of water, you may experience the curious phenomenon of interior mirage, whereby an image of the plunge bath appears in the corner of the sauna, looking cool and inviting (rather than it is like in reality: clammy, and crocheted by a thousand shed hairs). If you want to still further enhance the illusion, take a suitable book. I've spent many happy hours in the sauna at the Latchmere Leisure Centre in Battersea, reading T. E. Lawrence's *The Seven Pillars of Wisdom*, or Thesiger's *Arabian Sands*.

Alternatively, should you feel inclined to immerse yourself in the clammy fecundity of the rainforest, why not go in search of a steam bath? The very opacity of these artificial climates makes suspending disbelief that much easier. I often used to hang out in the Porchester Baths in Queensway of a weekend afternoon. This was in the days before it had been spritzed up and the upper level was carpeted a dun brown, wood-panelled, and equipped with old electroliers. Ranged along the sides of the broad chamber were curtained booths containing day beds, and from time to time an overweight East End cabbie would emerge from one of these, his moobs glistening with sweat, and join three of his colleagues at a baize-covered card table for a hand of brag. To complete the sensation of a seraglio populated

A LOAD
of BANKERS
SWEATING
IT OUT...

by hairy houris, there was a serving hatch at which you could procure such exotic sherbet as jelly and custard.

If you ventured downstairs there was the plunge bath, and beyond it no fewer than three steam baths, each foggier than the last. In the hottest and steamiest was enacted the ritual of the shmeiss, whereby the cabbies ritually scrubbed one another with a raffia brush dunked in hot, soapy water. Shmeissing was brought to the East End by eastern European Jews at the turn of the twentieth century, and it involved a definite ritual, while the shmeiss brush itself resembled a grass skirt. If you sat in there reading Lévi-Strauss's *Tristes Tropiques*, while the shmeissers bellowed and their brawny pink limbs floated in the vaporous haze, you could easily imagine yourself deep in the heart of the Amazon, with a bunch of Bororo crazed on yoppo.

For me, the sauna experience never fails to shift the weight of place. For years my favoured sauna was on the Finchley Road, next to the Cosmos Restaurant (where you could eat Wiener Schnitzel next to people who'd never, psychically, left Vienna at all). This outfit had the virtue of being open twenty-four hours a day, so that you could pitch up in the middle of the coldest night of the year, and stick your face in the hot crotch of Rio de Janeiro. Metaphorically, that is, because this was, and I believe still is, emphatically not an establishment where commercial – or any other – sex was available. Presumably, for those who savour such excursions *salace*, the trip to the anonymous shopping parade in the outer suburb, the step through the plate-glass door with its sign reading SAUNA, followed by the 'something extra' – a hand job under a thin towel – is as exciting as any other sex tourism.

The closest I've got to such experiences have been the rigours of professional massage. I've been pummelled in hammams from Fez to Cappadocia and back again – usually emerging feeling like pizza dough ready for the oven. There was the time I stayed at the famed Oberoi Palace in Delhi with the late Turnbull St Asser, and we thought to work off our narcotic excesses with a sauna and a massage. Everything went to plan up until the laying on of hands, which was accompanied by a liberal dousing in rosewater. Reader, he was a pretty boy, and I will forestall your blushes by saying that I was able to control myself as he manipulated me – exhibiting a stoic sexlessness that Thesiger would've recognised – by the simple expedient of imagining that I was on the Finchley Road.

# Longshore Drifter

I conceived the idea of walking from Flamborough Head to Spurn Head, along the Holderness coast of East Yorkshire. It was about forty-five miles and I could do it comfortably over three days. Why this walk along this coast? Well, the soil here – loess or clay – was deposited during the last ice age, and ever since then the long shore drift has been carrying it away to the south. The Holderness is, in point of fact, the fastest-eroding coast in Europe, with some six feet a year being lost to the North Sea.

I have distinct childhood memories of watching *Nationwide*, the BBC's evening TV current affairs programme, and seeing the folksy presenter, Michael Barratt, with his distinctive 1970s hairstyle (like an ice cream, melting asymmetrically over his brows), interviewing some poor householder who was sitting in one half of a room, while the other half had disappeared into a local void. 'I can't oonderstand it,' the householder was saying, with broad Yorkshire vowels. 'I oonly poot those UPV windows in laast year and now loook what's 'appened!' To which – I understood even aged twelve – the only possible reply was: 'Why the hell did you buy a house on the edge of a cliff, then?'

True, these may be screen memories of a screen – but the erosion was real enough. In January of this year there was a photo in the *Independent* of a house about to topple over the cliffs at Skipsea Sands, a third of the way along the coast, and that decided me: I would do the walk. I thought it would be strange enough seeing all these homeowners of the abyss, but stranger still was the notion that if I travelled the whole way within six feet of the cliff – or better still on the foreshore – I would be taking a walk that no one would ever be able to reproduce, because the very land itself would've disappeared within months.

Flamborough Head and Spurn Head are place names well enough known, as is the resort of Bridlington, but the rest of the coast – apart from its disappearing act

'ERE, MARGE! THOUGHT YOU SAID YOU BROUGHT ME A CUPPA TEA 'ALF AN HOUR AGO ?!!

TERRA INFIRMA

– has no public profile at all. Perhaps it was this constant erasure that made it so secret? Half a mile or more had gone since the Roman era, scores of towns and villages had been inundated since medieval times – could it be that such an ongoing diminution of once mighty – if always tiny – Albion was too much for us to face?

I left the train at Bempton and set off along roads, because there were no direct paths marked on the map. As ever under these circumstances I feared for my life: in rural England the walker and the driver are pitted against one another, flesh versus steel; and while pedestrians may be a little self-righteous, it's nothing to compare with The Divine Right of Cars. Still, the fields were full of ripening wheat, the hedgerows with brambles, there were larks in the sky and soon enough I reached the bird reserve at the end of Flamborough Head, turned south-west past the white-painted lighthouse and strolled along the grassy path beside chalk cliffs.

So far so conventional: cliffs a couple of hundred feet high, Bridlington with its Ferris wheel and roller-coaster standing out five miles away in the haze. I walked on at a brisk pace, the cliff ever declining, until I reached the outskirts of the Victorian town, and wandered, a strange revenant, through its holiday crowds: the young people eating fat and sugar, the old and obese sitting in their electric wheelchairs, one of which was blazoned 'Woodcock Assisted Mobility'. But beyond Bridlington things got – as Alice would say – curiouser and curiouser. Soon enough the bathers and sandcastle construction teams faded, the beach widened to half a mile or so, and there were men flying enormous kites, their parenthetic shapes bracketing sections of blue sky.

Flamborough and Spurn Heads were also shaped like two apostrophes, perhaps everything in between them was in quotes – or worse, ironised? There were concrete dragon's teeth strewn along the sands like the martial building blocks of gargantuan children, there were tip-tilting pillboxes on the bluffs above the beach, and quite suddenly I was entirely alone in all this sky, sand, loess and wheat.

I plodded on throughout the long, hot afternoon, while the chocolate bluffs mounted into cliffs and the concrete rubble on the beach grew and mutated. At about six I began to see the first struts and girders poking from the clay cliff, slippages of fresh earth marking the sign of recent falls, and sometimes sticking out from these, prosaic detritus: a sheet of galvanised iron, a roll of linoleum, a course of red bricks still mortared together – all of it instant archaeology. Chunky lumps of sea-rounded bitumen lay about on the beach, the biscuity remains of roadways dunked in the waves.

# The Erosion of Truth

If my first day on the Holderness coast was odd, the second was utterly bizarre. In the early morning the coast was blanketed in a sea fog – or 'fret' as they call it locally – and the dwellings along the cliff edge, which I now saw from behind, were ramshackle, winnowed out by the gulf opening up in their former front gardens. And yet, still people hung on here, despite the void encroaching beneath their feet. I headed south towards Hornsea, and passed through leisure park after leisure park, each one full of 'static' (ha!) homes.

I stopped to talk to one of these modern-day Canutes, a stocky man in a white singlet who was drinking a cup of tea on the tiny balcony of his caravan. I asked him if he was worried about the encroaching gulf, but he was blithe: 'When it gets too near they oop and move us back a few rows, like,' he explained. 'But we've forty-six feet between uz and the cliff – there's a chap in the next park along, he's only twelve, and his van 'nt even chained!' He shook his head at the idea of such folly then pointed out an embayment in the cliff between two promontories. 'See there, I reckon that'll be next to go, bit in t' middle went a few days ago.'

At Hornsea, snug behind its sea defences, I left the cliffs. All the inhabitants of the villages and towns along the Holderness believe that one settlement's defences – concrete bastions, steel groynes and floodgates – mean the next one along will be still more severely gouged. Certainly, as I trudged on I couldn't see much in the way of a beach until I reached Mappleton and descended into another world.

The cliffs here were high, and walking along beneath them I became fixated on the way the clayey mud mimicked everything from the finials and volutes of Gothic architecture to the physiognomy of the human face. The loess collapses either by being undercut by the sea, or due to what's called 'rotational slumping'. This looks exactly what it sounds like: the whole face of the cliff twisting round in response to some hideous torsion. When the cliff has fallen the next tide turns the chunks of clay into round blobs, each studded with multi-coloured pebbles.

Eventually, I met a fossicker, who stood and chatted to me with his hammer held at a jaunty angle while his kid smashed some blobs beside us with his. As we were talking there was a puff of earth along the beach and a section of cliff fell down, perhaps thirty feet across. 'You missed a really big 'un earlier on,' the fossicker said, not that he appeared in the slightest bothered; he was more interested in telling me that he once found the skeleton of a bison trapped in the clay. Then we parted – and I walked on, the mud pressing on my right side, for now, having seen a fall I was seriously anxious for the first time: what if I were to expire thus, humped by the frigid shoulder of Ceres?

The next day was still stranger. Waking just past dawn at the Old Plough Inn at Hollym, I could see that the sea fret was back – and thicker. I walked across the misty fields to the beach and set off for Spurn Head, the disc of the sun up above like a radiant vent around which the mist swirled. On and on crunching over shingle and coarse sand, with the only people about sea fishermen in ones and twos, trapped in their taciturn maleness. I got to Easington, and here were still bigger piles of old concrete blockhouses mangled on the beach. On I trudged, past the carefully roped-off breeding grounds of terns, which chirruped a warning overhead.

Then, I was there: I could see, even in the mist, Spurn Head stretching out ahead of me in the gloom, its spine covered in marram grass and furze, its shingle flanks speared with the rotting spars of failed breakwaters. The Head is three miles long, and constantly being eroded along its northern side, and reconstituted on the southern, which fronts the Humber estuary. I was gripped now - despite seriously blistered feet - with a fierce need to reach my destination, and then, as if to reward me, just as I passed the lighthouse, and the end of the promontory was in sight, the sea fret rolled back and the sun came out. I say 'the end', but if by this I mean a precise point, since Spurn Head is curved, I'm not sure that it was possible to establish the exact terminus of this parenthetic landmass. This noted, it could be, that like any other piece of quoted speech, I remain there still – together with my words.

# Against the Dying of the Light

In Ibiza the night proceeds according to plan: we set off in convoy, several cars full of us – true, we're going to a party in a swanky villa on the other side of the island, but while half our company are teenaged, the rest of us are past the age when we can do any raving – except against the dying of the light. Then: solid darkness, with headlights slicing through it to reveal switchback roads and useless signs. The mobile phone calls begin: the echolocation of decadent cetaceans. Some Ibizan parties can be found by following lizards stencilled on walls, others by pink balloons, but the turning for this one – or so we're assured through the ether – will be clear to us because of a strategically placed pile of three white phones.

'Phones!' Our radio operator-cum-navigator expostulates to general in-car hilarity. 'Three white phones!' she reiterates – and the mirth continues, until having driven the required kilometre back from San Miguel we find the pile of three white stones. If only we were – stoned, that is – but we're simply victims of a contact high as big as the island itself, a tenebrous and fizzing cloud of Methylenedioxymethamphetamine beneath which our hired Seat Ibiza struggles to gain purchase on the bumpy track.

Then, suddenly, I'm sitting at a poolside bar, drinking Coke and being talked at by a well-groomed posh hag in a see-through dress. Her arms are as brown as mahogany, her pupils as big as school pupils, her breasts are like the jowls of old men grafted on to her ribcage by psychotic surgeons. And she's drawling, 'Honestly, I was just setting off for the airport when that plane crashed . . . it couldn't've been a *worse* time, I mean, I absolutely *hate* flying.' It is, manifestly, all about her – not the 152 souls fried on the Madrid runway. 'I mean, I can *cope* with flying, but only with headphones on, my music playing, and absolutely *blotto* on Valium.'

Her name is Patsy Bunbury – or some such implausibility – and she, her banker husband, and a brace of Google-brained teens are all revolving around the party as high as kites that are about to crash into the ground: they jig and spin on the end of invisible strings of intoxication. It's very Ibiza, this, the transgenerational narcosis, and it gives the entire mise en scène – the pool with its artificial shingle beach; the enormous patio crowded with bohos, trustafarians and aristocrats; the trestle tables laden with truckles of tender beef – a certain Pompeiian air. You don't have to be a Cassandra to suspect that it's all about to go 'crunch', as the liquidity is sucked out of the revellers and they're left in their poses, freeze-dried for eternity.

The following day I decide to go for a walk around the northern cape of the island. This will be a modest five-miler in the thirty-degree heat, from Caló d'en Serra along the cliffs to Punta d'en Gat and the Caló des Pou, then on to the light-house at Punta des Moscarter. From there it looks to be a simple stroll down to the resort of Portinatx. However, nothing's ever as simple as that. My wayfinding – and that of my companion, Mark – is erratic. The underbrush is scrubby and thorny, the rocks are sharp. With many backtracks we make about a mile an hour. The Med sparkles, on the horizon the superstructure of a freighter piled high with containers wavers in the heat.

I begin to worry: will we become lost here in the Ibizan hinterland? Meeting perhaps with other Brits who've gone feral? A lost tribe of Bunburies, buck naked, who call themselves 'the E', and enact weird psycho-sexual rituals. Mark, on the other hand, is unconcerned, chatting away about how his dad made a fortune buying up ex-MOD Cold War bunkers in the Channel Islands, then growing mushrooms in them. And how weird is that?

Late that day I go to check on the teens who're bunking in a villa about a mile from where we're staying. The villa, as cubicular and white as a sugar cube, is called 'China White'. That's Ibiza for you – a not-so-funhouse mirror of Surrey, where premature retirees live in houses named after varieties of *heroin*. It's a beautiful evening, the sun lazily declining to the sea. From a villa down the hill float the hypnotic strains of a song that was ceaselessly played during my own summer of ersatz love: 'Fade Into You' by Mazzy Star: 'I look to you and I see nothing / I look to you to see the truth', the ethereal girl singer warbles her timeless existentialism.

And so you leave me, dear readers, on that Ibizan hillside, just as you leave Ralph fulminating in his Kentish atelier. For this is the last Psychogeography that we will ever pen. Au revoir, à bientôt, auf Wiedersehen – fade into you . . .

HOLY SHIT! THAT'S IT!!

WILL SELF and Ralph STEADman 26 Sept 2008